The Writing Room

Stories from the Lives of Callanwolde Writers

The Writing Room

Stories from the Lives of Callanwolde Writers

To my cousin Ann Marie
Love,
Jim Monacell

Editors
Sarah Kegley
Gretchen E. Maclachlan
Jim Monacell
Bill Moore
Lori R. Muskat

First edition, 2016.

The works collected herein are memoir, and are accounts as recalled and composed by the authors. In several instances names, places and other details have been changed in order to obscure identities while maintaining the essential truths portrayed.

Proceeds from the sale of this book benefit The Callanwolde Foundation's Scholarship Fund. The Callanwolde Foundation is a nonprofit organization advancing education in the arts and literature in Atlanta, Georgia.

ISBN 978-1-329-79459-7

DEDICATION

We, the students of Advanced Memoir Seminar, dedicate this anthology to June Akers Seese. We thank you, June, for sharing your talent with us and for helping each of us find our own voice. We couldn't imagine our writing or our lives without you.

Contents

Preface

I have always been interested in other people's business. I grew up behind a tall fence in a house with two books and lots of rules. There was a Bible used to record weddings and obituaries, and a well-worn copy of *Forever Amber* stuffed under my mother's mattress.

My parents worried a lot. "Mind your own business." "Don't put our business in the street." Yet they soaked up and shared all the neighborhood gossip. I was a quiet child who played marbles in the spring mud and listened, watched and waited for kindergarten. There I learned to read and never stopped. My library card grew so tattered I had to have it laminated.

I was drawn to stories in books, and I was fascinated by my father's tales from his Louisiana past. He had a sharp tongue. "Tell your troubles to Jesus," he once told a neighbor who thought she had him trapped with her life story as he painted our fence dark green.

It's no surprise that I became an English major in college. And, it's no surprise that my interest in the business of others influenced my writing and teaching. Nor that the memoir became the genre I now favor.

I have read so many books that my husband once told me, after eating a cold supper, "June, you lead a vicarious life." I laughed, looking at a tower of paperbacks on the floor. He responded by building a wall of bookshelves in almost every room. He was, after all, an English major, too.

After years of teaching the fictional process, in 2002, I went to Sam Goldman, Callanwolde's former Director. "All over the country, writing programs have added courses in the memoir to their offerings. Yale, Duke, even the New School for Social Research in Manhattan ..."—Sam cut me off before I got to Bennington. He told me to put some lesson plans and a blurb for the upcoming catalog on his desk before I left for the day. He also said the Music Room in the Mansion was free. Sam was not one to be left in the dust.

And so, *The Memoir — Reading It and Writing It* and then the *Advanced Memoir Seminar* have found their places in the Callanwolde Fine Arts Center catalog for the past thirteen years. Callanwolde has expanded and changed. The Samuel Goldman Retreat was built, and our class was invited to hold its annual November reading and champagne reception there. Two students have finished their memoirs and many others have published excerpts in literary magazines.

Then, five students from the seminar conceived of *The Writing Room: Stories from the Lives of Callanwolde Writers*, a collection of excerpts from their memoirs-in-progress. Over the course of a year, they solicited, selected, and refined the pieces, and melded them into this courageous book. They asked no help from me. "Just write the preface," they said. And so I did.

June Akers Seese

Introduction

We, the editors of this anthology and the authors collected herein, came together by way of different paths to study writing at Callanwolde Fine Arts Center. Through the tutelage of June Akers Seese, the creator of Callanwolde's memoir program and its instructor for the past thirteen years, we have learned that to write memoir and to write it well is nothing less than daunting.

June emphasizes in introductory classes that memoir is not a straightforward account. She writes: "A memoir is your story, your impressions .... In the end, it's a matter of light. It is as if the author stands outside a house at dusk with a flashlight and a tool box. He can shine his light on any window. The only rule is, once chosen, he must open it all the way and drag the reader in with him through the shadows to the deep, scary stuff. Otherwise he will be dealing in whitewash, not truth."

The question came simply enough, from one of us, one day after class: What did we think about publishing a collection of our work? With a resounding "yes," five of us agreed to serve as the editorial board.

The selections collected here are a sampling of the writings of seventeen authors who have completed Callanwolde's memoir seminars on one or many occasions, authors who have had the courage to drag their readers in, all the way to the shadowy corners. In roughly chronological order by the age of the protagonist, the stories present remembrances ranging from the authors' early childhood through late adulthood. As you turn the pages, you will find that nearly every aspect of personal experience is represented, from promise, regret, friendship, and sex, to doubt, loss, struggle, and expectation.

In making the selections for this book, we looked for authenticity in the accounts and power in the writing, and determined not to limit themes and tone. As a result, thoughtfulness, seriousness and humor abound in this varied collection. Yet, because memoir is reflection on life experience, common themes naturally emerge.

Prominent among these themes is the giving and withholding of love. The two opening selections are in a way bookends. In "Longing," Ellen Jones ponders how her mother could throw elaborate birthday parties for her and read *Br'er Rabbit* to her in dialect, yet be void of tenderness when it was most needed. In "Grandma Ruby," Shani Godwin shares a story of her grandmother who filled her belly full of hot dogs and her heart full of love. Lori Feig-Sandoval presents another dimension of love in "Sweet Tea," using her only child's exit on a red motorcycle to tell of the pain in letting go.

The struggle to find a place in the world inspires many memoirs. In Lori R. Muskat's "The Promise of Superman," a little girl searches for reflections of what she could someday hope to be. The teen years are prime for self-examination, and Paul Thim in "If You Knew" describes how his rock n' roll 45s opened in him new pathways in thought and feeling. Ralph Freedman's "Midwife to a Cow" provides a vivid moment in the journey of a political refugee.

Contrariness and contradiction are no less universally human. Robert Roth's anecdote about his childhood injury, "The Chicken that Broke My Arm," reflects family tensions and the ennui of youth. Park Morgan, in "An Affinity for Trouble," depicts the faults in his colorful but disreputable uncle, while describing himself following a similar path. And Sarah Kegley, in "Thin Soup," celebrates the joys of anonymity and unfettered time during her early months as an expat in Madrid, before new friends and responsibilities displace those elusive pleasures.

The authors also describe learning and growth. In "Facts of Life," Shelley Scher relates both a child's curiosity and first experiences of loss during one too-eventful summer. Chelsea Cook, in "Carl," illustrates how she came to learn, too late, that a man who may have been a crack addict was also her protector and her friend. Bill Moore recounts in "Swimming," how harsh expectations of a college coach propelled him to new achievements.

We all encounter in our lives evil, resolve and, hopefully, grace. These topics, too, are forcefully represented. In "Too Bright," graduating high-schooler Gretchen Maclachlan realizes her vulnerability as a woman when youthful pranks of classmates become serious threats.

Rebekah Durham, in "A Reluctant Evangelist," depicts herself as a college student, forced to confront alone the mysteries of sin and redemption. And in "Not for Whites Only," Don Bender shows that intimidation can be matched not only by faith, but by resolve.

Awakening and change probe our fears and yet inspire us. In "Sunday, Bloody Sunday," Lori R. Muskat recalls her first R-rated movie and early romantic longings. Gwen Filardi illustrates that aging produces strange transformations in "Good Golly, Aunt Lolly," the story of the rise and fall of an aunt's signature dessert. Finally, Jim Monacell writes in "Robin" of how a high school buddy's transformation challenged him to consider the meaning of friendship.

Regardless of what we each may have anticipated when we signed up for the first class, we could not have foreseen the impact of participating in June's seminars, the way our lives would be enriched, the way our viewpoints would expand, or the bonds we would form. We range in age from mid 20s to mid-90s, are gay and straight, of different cultures and ethnicities, and represent many of the world's major religions as well as most regions of the United States. In fact, despite the improbability that we would have met in any other way, we find that through our memoir classes we are securely fastened to one another, reinforced in our shared humanity through our writing. This anthology has been born of that experience.

We have shone the light into our open windows; we have inspected, exposed, shared, and pondered our questions onto the page. Through tears, laughter, and more than a little sweat we have found older and newer versions of ourselves, sometimes even making sense of the world we live in and the people around us.

And now, dear reader, we offer these stories to you. We speak as one in saying that we have enjoyed putting this book together as much as we have enjoyed the years of writing that preceded it. It is our collective hope that your chance encounter with these pages will leave you with a fuller heart, as ours has for each of us.

Sarah Kegley
Gretchen E. Maclachlan
Jim Monacell
Bill Moore
Lori R. Muskat

Atlanta, Georgia
March, 2016

Longing

The hardest thing about losing Dad was that I sometimes had him. When I was a kid, he'd take me for a jog once in a while before he went to work. He'd give me a hug or kudos on occasion. He'd let me lie on his bed watching movies with him as he lay dying. But for all of those things and anything more, I never had my mother.

Mom did read to my brother and me when we were little, books like *Br'er Rabbit,* in dialect. "Oh, puleese don't throw me in dat briar patch," she'd shriek. Since she liked animals, she also read *All Creatures Great and Small, Watership Down,* and *Ferdinand the Bull.* I particularly liked Ferdinand, since I too longed to be alone outside, smelling the honeysuckle on the back fence, swinging hidden behind the little backyard hill, singing the Beatles' "I Want to Hold Your Hand."

Mom read with great expression, her voice rising and falling as her fingers turned the pages. I smelled her perfume and watched her bosom rise and fall, and sometimes nestled my head near her shoulder. She used obscure, unwieldy words like "thwart" and "indefatigable," and when we asked their meanings told us, "Go look it up." But I wanted a mother who would flip through the dictionary with me, pull me closer, and hug me tight.

Once Mom told us how lonely she was as an only child and how she loved her cocker spaniel, Inky. I have a photograph of Inky standing with his hind legs on a black and white tile floor, front paws on the edge of a gleaming white bathtub, watching Mom bathe as a girl of three. Mom said she'd read for hours after bedtime under her covers with a flashlight. Books and Inky kept her company.

As I look back on those reading nights with Mom, I enjoyed the tales, even when I didn't always understand them. But I was on guard, as always, not warm and snuggled, not safe at my mother's side.

I used to slip into Mom's bedroom barefoot in my nightgown when she was getting ready to go out. She'd go about her business in her brassiere or draped in her satin robe, ignoring me huddled on the bench at the foot of her bed.

Mom would sit at her dressing table applying blood-red lipstick to her pooched out lips. She was always trying to make her thin lips larger. She'd squirt perfume on her neck and wrists and spray a cloud of Aqua Net around her immovable, fine brown hair. She'd wear cotton gloves to pull on her stockings. She would ask Dad's opinion as she opened jewelry drawers and held up pins and earrings. She would always get Dad to zip her dress and pin the diamond brooch on her breast, as she said her hands were too clumsy. Her knuckles were knotty, like mine, presaging arthritis. She would soak her rings in ammonia in a crystal ring holder by the bathroom sink. The smell wafted into the bedroom, caustic and overpowering. If I got too close it burned my nose. Finally, she'd rinse the ammonia from her rings, slide on the wet diamonds and sapphires, and squeeze their expandable bands to lock them in place. Then she was gone. The lingering smells were all that stayed with me.

Sometimes I'd see Mom in her office, bent over the sewing machine, working thread through holes and hooks with her awkward hands. Sometimes she'd rip out a hem from my brother's pants and sew a thinner one. Sometimes she'd pull one of Dad's socks over a wooden ball and darn it. I'd watch her across the hall from the door to my room, but I didn't go in. If I dared, I would feel lonelier because Mom would ignore me. Or worse, I'd feel crushed if Mom was feeling vicious. Better to keep my distance.

When my brother and I were needy, Mom would turn us over to nannies, "Mothers' Helpers," as she called them, or to the housekeeper Ruby, who cared for us during the day. Ruby would balance my legs on her thigh and wiggle my white socks with the lace trim on my feet, then pull out the toe end a bit and fold it under before sliding on my black patent Mary Janes. "That's so them toes don't get scrunched up in there," she'd say gruffly.

When I'd get home from school, Mom was usually in bed, and Ruby would be whooshing around in the kitchen while I'd get a snack. Lots of times I'd get a piece of white bread from the fridge and Ruby would look over her shoulder and spit, "You'd better *put* something on that bread."

Ruby wasn't one for hugging either, but I remember a few times when she gave me a quick squeeze about the shoulders. Once, as a teenager, when I was grappling with the aftermath of anorexia, I made the mistake of asking Mom, "Do I look okay?" I had a desperate mind and a depressed metabolism. I was losing control of the only thing I thought I could control, my weight. I needed reassurance, comfort, something to grab onto. Mom casually replied, "Well, your clothes would look better if you lost five pounds."

I went to my room gasping, and fell to my knees sobbing on my yellow pile carpet. My door was open as Mom strode past on the way to her room. Ruby trailed her with a load of towels. I heard Mom's door bang shut, then the linen cabinet click after Ruby stashed the towels inside. Ruby sidled into my room, me still slobbering on the floor, and stood over me. I could see her cheap white nurses' shoes and her bare heels standing on the backs, her own makeshift pair of clogs. I looked up past her ample belly and crossed arms as she said, with quick concern, "I hate to see you like this." Then she sighed and trudged out to take on another task or sit in the ironing room and listen to the radio by herself.

From as early as I can remember, Mom would leave me in a puddle after delivering a zinger. She'd turn on her heel and fling over her shoulder, "Sarah Bernhardt!" as she left the room. As a kid I didn't know what that meant, but I knew it wasn't good. Later, I looked it up: Sarah Bernhardt was a melodrama star. My mother used her name as a slur, a punctuation mark for each soul or character assassination she delivered.

When I was young, I had a Dutch Boy bob that didn't need much care. But as I grew to seven or eight, my blond hair fell to my shoulders and took a lot more work. It was fine and tangly, straight and glossy. I sprayed it with Johnson's No More Tangles after my bath, and combed it carefully, starting with the matted ends, unraveling the tighter knots.

When it was time for a picture or a birthday party, and Ruby wasn't around, Mom would come in, grab my brush, and make quick work of it. Starting at my forehead, she'd dig the bristles in and yank through to the ends. She'd gather the top into a rubber band, pulling the strands and twisting the band. Then around the band she'd tie a bow, usually red, her favorite color. My scalp would burn and I'd look in the mirror to see bumpy ridges in the pulled-back section. Sometimes my forehead strained at the tension, but I'd blink back tears and say nothing.

Mom was good at throwing birthday parties. I still have pictures of myself in a yellow or blue frock with the lace trimmed socks and Mary Janes, swinging at a piñata or watching a magic show in the backyard. Mom would get my birthday cakes from Rhodes Bakery: a fudge-cloaked layer cake bedecked with yellow roses and green leaves, or a Barbie doll torso sticking out of an icing-ribboned, yellow-cake skirt. One year Mom brought home a Baked Alaska from Baskin Robbins. She recounted to her friends how she kept dousing it in the kitchen with brandy and kept striking matches to it so she could bring it out in a blaze of flaming meringue glory. "I bet those children went home after that one and took *really* long naps," she snickered.

After I grew up and left home, Mom would call me on my birthday and sing the "Happy Birthday" song in its entirety. Then she would say, "I remember the narcissi were blooming on the beautiful spring day you were born. I prayed for a blond-haired, blue-eyed girl, and that's just what I got."

And that's when Dad started drinking more and all hell broke loose, I would add silently.

My birthday was the only time Mom would ever call me, except for the times she'd instruct me to do something for her. Those birthday calls befuddled me. Was she really glad I was born? Did I have it wrong?

After she died, I looked through her childhood scrapbooks. I found loads of photos from her own elaborate parties. Grandaddy was a gadget man, always tinkering with the latest technology in audio and visual recording, so he had taken stills and movies of Mom's fetes. My brother and I had watched the movies with him when we were young, on a pull-up screen with the curtains drawn and the reel-to-reel film flickering and jumping. We watched well-dressed children dining with starched napkins and silver, white gloves and ties. We saw Mom blowing out birthday cakes, swimming with friends in her backyard pool, twirling with a boy in a sea of friends, dancing to a band on the stage Grandaddy built in her upstairs playroom.

Just as later in life I made sense of Mom's reading to us as a soothing ritual from her childhood, having been unable to square my desolation with that cozy-seeming scenario before, I finally surmised that giving birthday parties also comforted her. When she read to us, or orchestrated parties, she could briefly relive her childhood, when she was the center of attention, before she had to scrounge for her husband's love, before she had to deal with his daily drunken tirades, before she had a daughter she saw as a threat, before she had children who needed from her what she didn't have to give.

When my youngest son was twelve, and I sat in a brown tweed room waiting for his aptitude testing to conclude, I saw a mother and teenage daughter enter and sit on the love-seat across from me. They chatted gently, smiling a bit, and the mother took the daughter's shoulder-length hair in her hands, caressing it, weaving it into a braid, then letting it go. My eyes started to spill, shocking me, and I had to leave the room. As I dabbed my mascara in front of the bathroom mirror, I thought of how my pitiful longing for Mom continues its insidious attacks. Even then, when I hated her.

Even now.

Grandma Ruby

Grandma Ruby was good at making two things—hot dogs and bacon. A plump lady with a laugh that rippled deep from within, my grandmother on my mother's side was the most eccentric person I have ever known. As a child, I looked forward to our frequent trips up I-85 headed north to visit Grandma Ruby in Cherryville, North Carolina. The small town situated just right outside of Shelby and Gastonia boasted a population that threatened 5,000. A small town that was still segregated for the most part by way of railroad tracks that separated the black folks from the whites, Cherryville was the epitome of country to me. To my mother it was home. My grandparents' shotgun house sat squarely on a busy highway that truckers used to conveniently whiz in and out of town. You see, Cherryville wasn't really a destination. It was simply a small town you passed through on your way to somewhere else.

For most of my childhood, an old dilapidated outhouse stood in my grandparents' backyard. A relic of a not so distant past, it was a symbol of the poverty my family had survived. To my mother, it was a reminder of colored water fountains, rides on the back of buses, and trips with Grandma Ruby to clean white folks' houses. To me it was just a worn down memory that littered the backyard. During those days, black folks were invisible. Knowing their place was the best protection they had against racism that coursed through the town as freely as water flowed from the spigot that stuck up from the ground in my grandparents' backyard. Cherryville was no different.

"Lord have mercy!" my grandmother would squeal as we walked through the front door. Tired and hungry from the four hour drive up from Atlanta, we'd shuffle in one by one as she greeted us at the front door. "I'm so glad y'all come!" With chest crushing hugs she'd smother us in her ample bosom, spank us on the butt and rush us into the kitchen. "How many hot dogs you want?" she'd ask.

For reasons unbeknownst to me, baking traditional Grandma-goodies like homemade cakes and pies never seemed to occur to Grandma Ruby. Instead, her specialty was hot dogs. Chicken franks of the boiled variety nestled in soft white buns to be exact. They were always waiting for us when we arrived and were ours for the taking—as many as our bellies could hold. When I was seven, she let me eat four hot dogs. One by one she'd serve them. "That was good Grandma Ruby," I'd say. Minutes later she'd return with another one. In fact, she would have allowed me to eat more if my stomach had not denied my greed. You see, she wasn't satisfied until you were full and content. In her house hot dogs were the way to her grandkids' hearts. While one would think she'd know better, as her grandchild I was glad she did not.

Years later, after her funeral, my cousins and I gathered in the tiny living room and each raised a hot dog in her honor. "You haven't had a hot dog," my cousin announced. "Until you've had a Ruby hot dog," we all proclaimed in unison and then we dissolved into laughter and tears as we reminisced and savored those last bites and memories.

So while my friends boasted about their big Thanksgiving meals and how great their grandmother's cooking would be, I shared stories of my own dear Grandma Ruby who filled my belly full of hot dogs and my heart full of love.

Grandma Ruby went to bed each night around seven p.m. and each morning you'd hear her clamoring around in the kitchen, way before sunrise, clanking pots and pans, banging around as if she was cooking a gourmet breakfast fit for a small village. In a shotgun house you can hear everything and my grandfather Daddy Dave did not take kindly to being interrupted at four a.m. by her morning rambling around. "Ruby, stop making all that damn noise," he would yell. "People in here trying to sleep." Her only response was more clanking and clamoring. Her only menu item was bacon.

Slowly the smell of bacon would fill the small house and she'd make the rounds stepping over her grandkids, daughters, and son-in-laws waking us each to take our order. "Shoney… ," she'd hover over me mispronouncing my name, "How many pieces of bacon you want?" Whispering loudly she'd continue insistently until I managed a groggy reply. "Huh, Grandma?"

"I'm making you some bacon, Shoney. How many pieces you want?" she'd repeat.

"Four pieces," I'd say, rolling over and returning to my dream.

As the sun would rise, we'd make our way into the kitchen to greet my Grandma who sat eagerly awaiting our arrival. With satisfaction in her eyes, she'd pile pieces of bacon onto our plates until we said "no more." There were never any eggs, no toast or jam to accompany it. Our parents would add the extras. And as we dove in, we'd thank Grandma Ruby with our appetites. I always looked forward to my grandma's bacon breakfasts, and truth be told I loved her hot dogs even more. Where else could a child revel in the love of her grandmother and bring joy to her heart simply by asking for seconds?

The Promise of Superman

Trying to figure out who I was supposed to be was like looking into those fun-house mirrors. In one, my face resembled an aging pumpkin that begins to sag two weeks after Halloween. *That's not me.*

In another, I was a human bowling pin of silly putty, stretched too far. *That's not me.*

And in the cruelest one, I actually thought I saw a reasonable likeness of myself—but only as long as I didn't move. For when I did, I came apart—arms, legs and head floating in search of a torso. Regardless, I somehow knew that I could not stay still just to maintain the appearance of being whole.

Perhaps that's when it first began, my talent for immersion in activity. My mother always said that when I sat for too long or lay down voluntarily, she knew I did not feel well. Ironically, it is probably truer that when I was moving,

I could not feel at all—and that was precisely the point. Motion soothes the ache; activity keeps the monster at bay.

Then there was television. Television offered reflections too. Reflections of a world with women starched beyond recognition and men who could fly.

Some mornings I watched *Leave It to Beaver.* Despite the potential meaning of her last name, Beaver's mom, June Cleaver, was not exactly someone to be feared by most. But she scared the shit out of me. Her blonde hair with each strand in its place, her stiff, wrinkle-free dress, her pristine home, the brownies that never burned, and that awful smile etched across her too perky face. As far as my five-year-old mind could tell, my life's purpose was to someday prance around a spotless kitchen in a big dress that barely moved, thankful to be alive and able to cook perfect meals for my husband and sons who were actually allowed to go out of the house. I had no choice but to run away as fast as I could and to keep running.

Afternoons held the promise of Superman, and he was an entirely different story. I'll admit that I hated the way Clark Kent slicked his hair back, and I always thought his eyeglass frames were too large for his face. I found him overly patient with Jimmy Olsen, too meek with Perry White, and I really never got the flirtation with Lois Lane. It's not a choice I would have made. But no matter, once he took off those nerdy eyeglasses and donned that skintight outfit with the flowy cape, Superman was way cool—even with the slicked back hair.

So, it's probably no surprise that one of my favorite photos of myself from 1963 is the one taken in the kitchen of our apartment in Newark, New Jersey. I'm wearing white underpants with a white undershirt tucked into them, and I've got my towel cape secured with a safety pin around my neck.

Standing on a kitchen chair of cracked vinyl, I'm ready to take flight.

You can't blame me for being black and white about things back then. It was the motif of the times. Racial tensions were smoldering. It was also the way of a child's mind. And the monochromatic images of June and Clark did little to challenge it.

What was I then? What am I now? Let me try to explain. I was a Clark Kent kind of little girl in a world that wanted me to be June Cleaver. In many ways, I still am.

Facts of Life

My mother was a prude. Even after having two children, me being the second, she wouldn't discuss anything that had to do with sex. When I was six, I noticed a woman who was so pregnant that she was walking from side to side and holding her back. I turned to my mom and asked, "How will the baby get out?" I had guessed the baby could crawl through the mother's mouth, but this baby looked so big that I couldn't quite imagine the possibility. The thought of cutting the baby out didn't occur to me. I had seen *Gone with the Wind* and Mellie screamed a lot but Scarlet didn't bring in any knives. I was prepared for anything but what I got. "I will tell you later," Mom replied.

Two days later my education began. Mom had gone to the library and brought home books. I was already reading but the words in *Dick and Jane* didn't prepare me for the vocabulary in these library books. There were seven books;

Mom spared no knowledge as long as I would not ask her to speak the words.

As I recall, reading the few words I could decipher brought me no understanding. Even the pictures didn't really help. They showed parts of the woman's insides with a big baby, still stuck right there, with no way out. The baby's head was pointed downward, but that tunnel was even smaller than my mouth. Eventually the books went back to the library. I didn't ask my mother any more questions about childbirth. After all, most kids can tell when their parents aren't going to give them the answers.

In third grade, I made friends with a girl named Grace, who had been left back. Grace was older, and we all thought she knew everything about "sex." She told me where the baby came out and about how it stretched and other stuff. I didn't think Grace could be right. I went home and pulled on myself to see how far my vagina would stretch. Although I didn't believe Grace, I wasn't going to let her know, just in case. Anyway, Grace was much more interested in how the baby got in.

She warned me that I should never go into a dark parking lot with a boy. She explained that boys carry balloons and they blow them up. If they insert them into your pants, you get pregnant. This procedure truly baffled me. Having no way to confirm or deny and seeing all the other girls nodding their heads as Grace told the tale, I suspected it was true. Yet, I was still uncertain and confused.

In December of the year I turned twelve, my father had a heart attack and died. His death did not seem real. "You are very brave," I was told by countless relatives and neighbors, as I passed out tissues and hugged my distraught mother. I did not cry and I did not grieve.

Dad's death brought many changes. Right after he passed, my fourteen-year-old cousin Neil, along with his father, my Uncle Sammy, came to help my mom pack up our house. Neil and I really had fun and felt a special cousin connection. I still didn't know much about the sex thing. One day while we were walking through the trees in our back yard, he asked me if I knew the "facts of life." I told him Grace's theory. Neil said that wasn't true and that he would tell me if I wanted to know. I had yearned for this information for so long, but for some reason I wasn't sure I still wanted to know. Of course, my curiosity got the better of me.

Neil said that first both mom and dad took off their clothes. I stopped him right off. I supplanted his false theory with my fresh information.

"But my mom undresses in her closet."

He insisted this was different. It happens at night in their bed. This possibility was really hard for me to digest.

"You mean, there's no balloon?"

"Not that I know of," Neil laughed. I kept his information to myself. I had a hard time imagining my parents in bed naked. It kind of changed the way I looked at my mom.

After dad died and mom sold the house they had built together, we moved to New York. For about six months we lived with my cousin Neil and his family, and I really enjoyed our friendship. Neil and I would attend Broadway shows together. We'd take the train into New York City, eat at Jack Dempsey's—where it was rumored stars would eat— and then walk over to the magnificent side streets off Broadway that housed the Broadway shows. After the show, we would wait outside for the stars to come out so that we could collect their autographs. Then we would return to Long Island on the railroad. If all of this wasn't magical enough, Neil would spin the vinyl record album of the show tunes from our adventure on his turntable, and we would create our own interpretations of the dances. He would twirl me in the air, lift me up, and hold me above his head while I posed in many graceful positions.

When we were not visiting the incredible New York City, we would stay home training our parakeets. We had bought them together at the local pet store. His was blue; mine, yellow. We made them stay on our shoulders and taught them to switch shoulders upon command. The summer days passed quickly. I thought about Dad a lot.

One day we found a baby bird that had fallen from its nest and broken its wing. We put it in a padded box and placed it near the furnace for warmth. We took turns feeding it sugar water through an eyedropper. We nursed that baby bird, but we woke one sad morning to find it absolutely still in its padded box.

By the end of the summer, Mom had found an apartment and we prepared to leave. When I said good-bye to Neil, I knew he had taught me a lot but I had learned some things myself. That summer I learned how babies escaped and that fathers, like baby birds, just didn't always stay.

The Chicken That Broke My Arm

When I was old enough to ride my bicycle in the street, my mother would send me on errands in the summer. Usually, these were short runs to the nearby Food Fair grocery store on Alton Road, a few blocks from our apartment.

Late one Friday afternoon, I came home tired and dirty from a hard day of play with my friends.

"Bobby," my mother yelled from the kitchen when she heard the door, "I need for you to ride over to Beach Poultry on your bike and get a chicken."

"I'm tired," I answered. "Make dad go."

"He doesn't feel well."

"Can't you cook something else? Why do we have to have chicken? I don't even like chicken."

"We're having chicken." She picked up a five dollar bill from the kitchen counter and held it out to me. "Here's the money. Make sure you get a done one."

"I don't want to go."

"Don't argue."

"But, mom ..."

"Just go."

Beach Poultry was about 15 blocks from our apartment. It wrapped around the corner of Espanola Way and Euclid Avenue. It was where you went for a rotisserie chicken. Practically every kosher chicken consumed in Miami Beach came from there.

The store was crammed full of giant rotating rotisseries loaded with chickens in different stages of cooking. There were no outside walls to Beach Poultry, just wide archways and pulldown metal doors. At dusk, the arches and the amber glow from all the rotisseries gave the place a Moorish atmosphere.

I didn't want to go. But it looked like I had no choice. I snatched the money from my mother and slammed the front door on my way out.

I was still pissed when I got to Beach Poultry. I paid the guy and tossed the chicken, wrapped in butcher paper and still warm, into the front basket of my bicycle and started home. I wasn't ready to turn loose of my anger yet; nursing it felt too good. Muttering to myself, I slowly peddled the bike, looking down at the road most of the time.

It came out of nowhere. A loud crash. So fast and startling, I had no idea what had happened. Everything just stopped, and I was lying in the street.

There was a man shouting at me. "ARE YOU OK?"

Dazed, I looked up at him from the street. "My arm hurts," I moaned. Then my head began to clear a little. "My chicken," I said. "Where's my chicken?"

It was lying next to my bicycle, which now had a crumpled front wheel from crashing into the man's open car door. I'd have to walk it home. I stood up, righted the bike, yanked the wire basket back into shape, and put the chicken in it. Other than a few small tears and dirt smudges, the butcher paper was intact.

"Are you okay?" the man asked again.

"I've got to get home," I said, and began wheeling my broken bike away. It was slow going. By the time I reached our apartment house, my arm was swollen and throbbing.

My mother and father were in the kitchen. I placed the package on the counter. "Here's your chicken," I said. Then I held up my swollen arm for them to see, "I broke my arm to get it."

If You Knew

The excitement is there immediately in the rapid pulsing of the sixteenth notes on the tom-tom and bass guitar—*dah*-dah-dah-dah *dah*-dah-dah-dah, *dah*-dah-dah-dah *dah*-dah-dah-dah— and then the tension between the tempo of the drummer and the slower, but still brisk, tempo of the singer. The words simple and clear, gliding over the—"If you knew, Peggy Sue, then you'd know why I feel blue ..." At the end of the verse the words catch up with the drum—"*Pritty*-pritty *pritty*-pritty-*Peggy* Sue."

It is 1957, I am ten years old, and my 45 rpm record costs eighty-five cents. I've been listening to music on the radio and asked my parents for a record player, and Dad took me to a store where a man he knew sold us one with the words "High Fidelity" on it. In my attic bedroom there is a simple, white wooden chest full of toys, but the toy chest is closed now and my record player is open on top of it. I am playing my records and replaying them and then playing them again, taking in the music and the singing. I notice how Buddy Holly sings one verse of "Peggy Sue" in a high pitched child's voice and then another verse in an exaggerated low voice, as though singing to a child. I am making sure I understand each word of the songs on my records. I am also taking in the labels on the records.

The label of "Peggy Sue" is coral colored and has on it, in large print, the word "Coral," which is also the name of Buddy Holly's record company. The labels of my records tell me how long each song is, in minutes and seconds, and under the singer's name are names in parentheses of the songwriters, all of which I linger over.

A record with the green label of Groove Records brings me the alluring voice of Sylvia Robinson, "You're sweet *l-o-v-ing* ... is better than a *kiss*. When you *l-e-a-ve* me ... sweet kisses I *miss*." I replay that record for a month, paying attention to how Sylvia ends the word "miss" abruptly, and in the momentary pause after that word—in the absence of sound—I feel the loss she is singing about. And I let Mickey Baker's guitar solo have its effect on me, beginning with four ascending notes, the fourth one drawn out, hanging, as though anticipating and reliving the loss—"Bow, bow, bow, *Bowww*"—followed by four quick descending notes— "Bu-Bu-Bow-Bow"—and then the rest of the solo, simple, repetitive and light, lifting the spirit out of the pain of loss.

"Love is Strange" is a song of romantic love, something I have not really experienced at age ten, although in third and fourth grade, before I ever listened to Mickey and Sylvia, I did have a girlfriend. Every day Laura Wilson wore her hair pulled back neatly into two braids, each tied at the end with a brightly colored ribbon. The other boys and I thought she was the prettiest girl in our class, and once a year I passed a note to her that read, "Dear Laura, I love you. Do you love me? Please check." There were two boxes on the bottom, one labeled "Yes," one labeled "No," and for two years she checked "Yes." After fourth grade, Laura moved out of town, and I became interested in the next prettiest girl, Kathy Dubin. Just a fourth grader, but I was putting a toe into deep water.

Now at age ten, I am venturing into deeper water, only I am focused not on a pretty girl with braids but on my records. I am immersing myself in them, trusting these things that I am discovering in the world around me and trusting what I am discovering inside of me—how the opening notes of "Peggy Sue" excite me and how Sylvia Baker's singing speaks to me about love and loss. I am letting myself go with it and discovering—when Mickey Baker's guitar solo transforms the pain of loss into something soothing—that if I let myself go something more can come out of it. In the safety of my attic room and my records, I am rehearsing for life.

I have other records I listen to repeatedly. The first one I ever bought is a 78 rpm of Elvis' "Hound Dog" and "Don't Be Cruel," which has the black label of RCA. Years from now some of us will consider that the perfect place to begin. The songs I am responding to are songs of excitement, exuberance and joy; they are about love and longing, about sex and heartbreak. They are also about other things, but I don't know that now. I will learn later that "Hound Dog" was originally recorded by Big Mama Thornton, a black singer who made a lot less money on her recording than Elvis did on his. Still later I will learn the song was written by two Jewish men, Jerry Lieber and Mike Stoller. Another record I listen to over and over again is "Party Doll" by Buddy Knox and the Rhythm Orchids. (Roulette Records, a yellow and orange label in a roulette wheel pattern.) It's rockabilly and I am hearing a hybrid of country music and rhythm and blues. It is as though my records are showing me a map of places I have not yet visited—experiences to be had, things to be learned—that are in the world out there, beyond the street where I live.

The name of the street where I live is Thornton Street. Like all the streets in my neighborhood—Wakefield, Elgin, Greenway, Ardmore—it sounds like it could be the name of a street in England, and the names of many of the families on our block seem to fit with the street names: Jordan, Clark, McDowell, Hill, and, of course, Smith. Some of the family names reflect a more diverse history. The Marx family and Mrs. Reichel, with their Germanic names. The Cusano's, with their six children, live directly across the street from us and are Italian. Louie Schneiderman's family is Jewish, and I know that Molly Adrianapolis' name is Greek. From my neighborhood friend Tony Grillo I learn that Italians can be called wops and guineas and that his uncle calls a Cadillac a Jew canoe. There are no families in our neighborhood that my parents have taught me to refer to as Negro or colored, but nevertheless I learn they are also called niggers and coons. Growing up on Thornton Street, we are aware of those distinctions and differences, but we also believe—we *know*—they are manageable.

A year after listening to "Peggy Sue" in my attic room, it's a Sunday morning in 1958, and I am sitting in church next to Robert Kruglick. He is whispering to me so that he won't get caught—something about "*Do*-you-Do-you, *Do*-you-Do-you," and I hear the word "dance." I don't understand what he is talking about, but I know he's excited about it. Listening to the radio a few days later, I hear the song he was talking about: "*Do*-you-Do-you-*Do*-you-Do-you—Do you wanna *daa*-a-ance. Oh, *Baaa*-by, do you *wanna* dance." It's not the later tongue-in-cheek version by the Beach Boys, but the original by Bobby Freeman, who sings it like he means it, and now I'm excited, too.

I have no way of knowing that in the years ahead life will be unmanageable and love will be painful in ways I cannot imagine and that, in still other ways I cannot imagine, I *will* manage my life and I *will* find love. And I have no way of knowing that almost sixty years from now I will occasionally hear "Love Is Strange" on the radio or in a store, and Mickey Baker's guitar solo will lift my spirit, and I will enjoy the banter between Mickey and Sylvia:

> Sylvia, how do you call your lover boy?
> I say, "Come here, lover boy!"
> And if he doesn't answer?"
> I say, "Oh, lover boy ..."
> And if he *still* doesn't answer?
> I say ...

And off Sylvia will go into a full-throated, drawn out "B-A-A-A-B-Y, my sweet B-A-A-A-B-Y..." And I will go off with her. And I will feel that life is safe and good and manageable.

Oh baby.

Sunday, Bloody Sunday

Union Center was a favorite destination once we were old enough to take the bus there alone. The main intersection of Morris and Stuyvesant Avenues was a busy one, and Mom always reminded me to be careful when crossing it. Just off the corner, there was the movie theatre where we paid fifty cents to see a double feature. I saw the Beatles' *Yellow Submarine* and *Help* there. I also saw my first R-rated movie there with Martha—*Sunday, Bloody Sunday*. By that time, double features had gone up to seventy-five cents—although an occasional special feature might have cost that much by itself.

Sunday, Bloody Sunday caught my attention for two reasons. One was Glenda Jackson. I have no idea how I even knew who she was, but I did—and she had become my favorite actress.

The other was that Martha and I had heard that the movie was about a young guy who was bisexual and had feelings for both Glenda Jackson and this male physician who was much older than he. I'm sure we were hungry for anything to help us make sense of the deepening attraction between us, still unspoken.

Neither Martha nor I looked anywhere near the eighteen years old we needed to be to get into an R-rated movie. I barely looked eighteen when I turned twenty, let alone when I was fourteen. So we were sweaty-palmed and giddy as we rounded the corner from Morris to Stuyvesant and approached the theatre box office.

As we stepped up to it, seriousness bordering on gravity crept across our faces, and we stood up straighter. That would make us look older. A woman wearing tortoiseshell half glasses and a crewneck apricot sweater with fake pearls sat behind the glass. She looked bored and seemed startled to see us, as though her boredom was preferable. She forced a librarian's smile. "Can I help you?" Martha, in front of me in line, said in a flat voice "One for *Sunday Bloody Sunday*, please." A thick silence, which couldn't have lasted more than a few seconds but seemed like an hour, filled the air. My heart was pounding so heavily, I could feel it pulse in my temples.

My thoughts raced. What if one of our classmates walked by and noticed we were going to see a movie together? Worse yet, a movie about bisexuality? What if the box office lady had a secret button that summoned the police when underaged teens tried to get into an R-rated movie? What if one of my mother's friends walked by? Or worst of all, what if my mother's mah jong group saw me here?

By this time in my life, my mother's mah jong group was well-established as my conscience. Mah jong is kind of like a cross between dominos and a card game that's played with tiles which have Chinese characters. How a game that

originated in China was kept alive primarily by Jewish women
in the U.S. is not exactly clear. But most Jewish kids growing
up in the suburbs in the 60s and 70s had moms who played
mah jong weekly in groups of five women. And most can
recall the clanking of the tiles punctuated by voices calling
out weird names like "three bam," "two crak," and
interspersed with raucous laughter. My mom's game was on
Tuesday nights, and I dubbed her group "the Tuesday night
five."

It was as though there was this little room in my brain
with a slatted wooden door on creaky spring hinges. Behind
that door, four of the Tuesday Night Five—Nan Steinman,
Myra Finkle, Pearl Poschnitz and Heddy Katzman—sat
around a card table with a single light bulb and one of those
pan-like tin covers suspended above it. Whenever I did—or
sometimes even thought about doing—something I wasn't
supposed to, the creaky door swung open, and out they
marched single file, dressed in coordinating polyester
pantsuits to stalk me and report back to my mother.

Images of the mah jong group faded with the ringing
of the movie theatre cash register and the *click-click, click-
click* of the ticket machine. The woman, eyes glued to the
ticket, tore it off and handed it to Martha, who walked up to
the glass doors to enter the lobby. Struggling not to show my
relief and excitement, I stepped up to the window, still aware
of my pulsing temples and hoping that their throbbing was
not visible. I focused on the bridge of the woman's glasses
and noticed that her eyebrows were half real and half penciled
in. Trying to match Martha's delivery, I too said in a flat
voice, "One for *Sunday Bloody Sunday*, please." Averting my
gaze to the small round hole in the pane, I reached into the
pocket of my burgundy bomber parka and pulled out a
wrinkled dollar bill. I tugged at the ends and smoothed it out

33

with my thumbs as I had seen my mother do, before placing it in the metal tray beneath the cut-out in the glass. As she had with Martha, the box office lady looked only at the ticket in her hands as she pushed it under the cut-out. I said thank you, turned slowly, took a step, pulled open the heavy glass door and stepped into the lobby. Looking at the maroon carpet speckled with bits of candy wrappers and errant popcorn kernels, I handed my ticket to the usher, who wore a uniform that made him look like an organ grinder's monkey. He tore my ticket, placed one half of the stub through the slit in a square grey box that sat atop a wooden pole and gave the other half to me. I stuffed it in my pocket. Martha greeted me with an oversized Chunky she had bought me, as we maintained our serious expressions in case we were under surveillance. The *pop, pop—pop, pop* and smell of fresh popcorn followed us as we walked into the already darkened theatre. We chose an empty row about halfway to the front and settled into our seats.

"I told you we'd get in," Martha whispered with a smile in her voice and elbowed me in the ribs. My side felt warm where she had touched me, and I was glad it was dark. She was right. She did tell me we'd get in. She was always more daring than I was. We might have both had the same idea, but she was always brave enough to say it. I loved adventure, but I didn't want it to be my idea. She'd give a small tug on my sleeve, and I'd follow her anywhere— although I don't think she knew that.

I wished my heart would stop pounding. I was scared that Martha would feel it through the cushions of our attached seats. She reached into her pocket to get out her box of Raisinets and her arm brushed against mine on the armrest. Tingles shot clear from my shoulder all the way into my fingertips, and I pulled my arm close to my side. Martha rattled some Raisinets out of the box and held them in her open hand that she pushed toward me. I hesitated.

"You want one?" she whispered, moving her mouth so close to my ear that I could feel her breath. I imagined my ear melting and dripping off my head into a messy little puddle on the floor.

"No thanks," I whispered back, maintaining a safe distance.

"But I thought you liked these."

"I do."

"Then have some."

"Maybe, later."

A woman in the row in front of us, whom I hadn't noticed, shifted in her seat and shot us a glare. Martha looked at me with a smirk and one raised eyebrow, and I knew what was coming next, as she held her middle finger up close to the back of the woman's head. We shook with silent giggles, channeled through our nostrils so that we sounded like two sniffing dogs. We then turned toward one another and mimicked the woman's pissy expression. Sniffing giggles gave way to gasping snorts, which drew another glare from our neighbor. I lurched forward in my seat, my belly sore and I squeezed my legs together, stifling a strong urge to pee. Looking away from Martha, I had to think about my grandmother being dead and other sad things to keep from laughing out loud.

Disaster averted, I sat up and settled back into my seat. Martha had also settled down and rattled more Raisinets into her hand, pushing it toward me.

"I'm gonna want some of your Chunky," she whispered.

"Okay. But I don't want to open it yet."

"I know, but I want some when you do."

"Okay."

"So have some of these."

I felt for the Raisinets in her hand in the dark.

"Ooh," her hand jumped a little.

"What!?"

"That tickles."

"Sorry."

"It's okay. Here."

She took several Raisinets and placed them in the palm of my hand. They were warm from her hand so that the chocolate coating left a film on my fingers and melted away from the raisins as soon as I put them in my mouth. I licked the chocolate off of my fingers as the opening credits began to roll.

Now, I started to fret as I remembered that I was about to see my first R-rated movie. Was I about to pass a threshold that would change me forever? What if I forget to lie and tell my parents the real name of the movie? What if the film raters were right, and this movie has something in it that I am too young to see? And what might that be? It's probably something sexual. But I knew what all the body parts look like; I'd known that for a long time from *Playboy* and from some hard porn magazines that one of my friends had pilfered from her older brother. I'd also read descriptions of sex in *The Godfather* and *The Fan Club*, when Helen Mastronardi and I used to raid her mom's nightstand while she was at work. We'd even found rubbers in her brother's dresser drawer one time—although we didn't think he had really *done it*. I thought I understood how all the parts worked and fit together—although I'd never *really* seen people having sex. Not even in the porn magazines. That must be it, I thought. This movie must have sex scenes. I'm about to see sex, I thought.

Just then, I heard the creaking door and the familiar cackle of my mother's mah jong group.

Carl

"You usin' that timer raht now?" Carl pointed at the electric timer attached to the industrial oven.

"No," I responded. "Next batch doesn't go in for a couple hours."

"Perfect!" He walked over and set it for 30 minutes.

"Now, Chesley, when this timer goes off, you just walk 'bout haff way down the cellar stairs and call out 'til I respond. You don't gotta come down heyuh, just call out."

"Uh ... okay. What if someone asks me where you are?"

"Tell 'em you just dohn no."

Carl was the head dishwasher at Atlanta's Flying Biscuit Café where I worked for three years in high school. I say "head" dishwasher because he seemed to have accumulated more respect than the other guys who filled in every once in a while. He had more respect, so he got away with more shit. Like taking 30-minute breaks in the cellar.

For months, I was scared about what he was doing down there—he had the telltale teeth marks of a crack smoker. But surely a family brunch spot—even in the cellar—wasn't his crack den of choice. I was even more scared about what he was doing down there if he *wasn't* smoking crack. He was as friendly as could be, but having grown up in Midtown, it wouldn't have been my first encounter with a man masturbating, and I sure as hell didn't want to have a second. One day, a toilet overflowed in one of the bathrooms. The pipes were the same ones from when the space was built in 1910, and no waitress was ever up for the job. Carl was the go-to man, and he wasn't responding to my usual "Caaaarrrr-uulll" calls down the stairwell. I had to suck it up, creep down those stairs and get him.

My laughter woke him. I'd found him comfortably horizontal atop a three-sack high, four-sack long stack of organic rolled oats. His dreadlocks, free from his hairnet, flopped over the sides and he used a dirty apron as his blanket. His boots were tucked neatly next to the gallon jugs of soy sauce. His face, open-mouthed and snoring, was juxtaposed with the face of a giggling baby on the oatmeal packaging, enjoying breakfast with only two bottom teeth.

What the management tolerated baffled me. Carl would often keep his 64-oz. plastic Quick Trip cup right next to the dumping sink in the dish pit. As servers and busboys would walk up to unload their armful of dirty dishes, he'd call out: "Any akk-a-hol ya got, any akk-a-hol a'tall, just po' it in dis cup."

"But Carl, this was like ... a pretty spicy Bloody Mary," I said the first time he asked me to do this.

'I don't care none, just po' it raht in dat cup."

After a while, he didn't have to remind us, if the cup was there, we po'd it in. "Carl's cup," we called it— and at the end of the night, he'd guzzle down that 64-oz. concoction of red wine, beer, Mimosas, Bloody Marys, Irish coffees, white wine and margaritas, and let out a big belch.

Sure, he had some peculiar behaviors, but he was someone I really began to trust. That's the thing about working in restaurants—you think everyone you work with is crazy, or close to it. They often can't find work anywhere else, or they're artists, resentful that they are expending their energy working instead of creating. But even with all the crazy, you develop a deep and loyal relationship with some of your coworkers, because you see each other in vulnerable situations—serving others—and know you're destined for something better.

If I was studying for a test, or crying over a boyfriend, Carl would often sweep and mop the bakery for me and let me go home early. I lived right by the restaurant in Candler Park, just a short walk away. Oftentimes I'd have to be at the restaurant by 6 a.m. on weekends to open a brunch shift. If I'd sleep through my alarm, Carl would run across the street and bang on my bedroom window, and say, "Getcha ass up, sweetie. Deez yuppies need dey cawfee!"

My parents would give him $20 here and there to wash their cars or mow our front lawn. When we put in a driveway, my stepfather gave him $100 to help us shovel and spread the gravel.

When I was sixteen, I saved $3,000 to buy a used Volkswagen Jetta. It was a piece of shit, but when I brought it home he ooo'd and aaw'd like it was a Cadillac. Sometimes I'd get off work and see he'd gone over and washed it for me. Sometimes I'd give him a ride home down Moreland after closing shifts—it wasn't a long walk, but if it was raining or cold, he'd always ask. And I'd usually say yes. He told me that he had two kids, probably my age by now, but that he wasn't allowed to see them. "Addiction's like cancer," he'd say. I told him a lot about my dad's struggles with addiction and jail time, but I don't know whether that made things better or worse, because Carl knew how much I blamed my dad for our poor relationship.

One time I called in to the restaurant saying I was going to be late because I got a flat tire in my high school parking lot. Carl walked sixteen blocks to meet me and help me change the flat, and wouldn't accept the cash my mom offered when I got home.

A customer once swatted my ass as I walked away with his drink order. I wasn't sure how to handle it, but when word made it back to Carl, he followed the man out to his car and screamed at him. I asked Carl what he said. "Don' eeeeven worry about it—dat man jus' needed to know you is a CHILD. A sixteen year ol' CHILD."

When it was near time for me to leave for college, things with the Flying Biscuit's management and me were falling out—I was blowing off my shifts and calling in sick a lot. I wanted to drink beer and sneak out late at night with my friends. I wanted to skinny dip in neighborhood pools after hours. I was ready to get out. And I never said goodbye to Carl.

I've been in there several times since moving back and caught up with the astonishing number of servers and cooks who still work there. Paula, who works weekend brunches and is a stay-at-home mom during the week; Jeffrey, who everybody calls Dewberry, who had lap band surgery and lost 150 pounds but is quickly gaining it back; KellyO, an aspiring actress who now has her own web-series and has been in a few commercials; J.P., who's started his own production company focusing on gory horror and zombie flicks. But no Carl.

Carl

No one knows where he is. Nobody knows why he just didn't show up for work one day.

Nobody ever said this out loud, but everyone was thinking it: no one knows if he's even still alive.

RALPH FREEDMAN

Midwife for a Cow

In 1939, just before the beginning of World War II, the British allowed young German-Jewish refugees into its country as "agricultural trainees." I was then nineteen years old and was placed with a farming family in the British midlands near Buxton, Derbyshire. This dairy farm was where I, a city boy from Hamburg, spent two years as a farm worker.

I loved working with the dairy cattle and came to recognize their breeds and temperament while I was learning to operate the milking machine. Another of my farm tasks was to clean the cow sheds after milking when the animals were let out to return to pasture. As the water splashed over the floor, gushing from the long black hose, I waded in the muck, pushing the heavy broom, amid the dank smell of cow dung.

I will never forget having acted as a midwife to one of my favorite cows, Number Six, the Ayrshire. This young cow calved with great difficulty. Most of the farm's adults stood around the flickering lamp in the barn—there was the boss, his wife, and his father while I scurried back and forth, carrying warm water from the kitchen which the family's Grandmother kept on producing all night long. I ladled water from one bucket to another for the farmers to use in helping the poor cow with her labor pains. How she bellowed!

Hers was a breech birth and someone or something was needed to right the calf. The veterinarian, a pleasant young fellow in his late twenties, asked me to reach the calf deep in its mother's belly. I was able to help with the delivery because, having grown up in a city, my arms were thinner than most boys. The veterinarian made me disinfect and soap my right arm all the way up to my armpit before I plunged inside. All the while he praised me, as if I too needed to be soothed and encouraged. I still feel my hand trying to hold on to the tiny slippery foot inside the mother.

It seemed to take endless time before I could grasp the hoof deep in the interior swamp. It kept sliding away, back into the suffering animal's body. The calf was stuck, unable to budge. In my despair, I focused my eyes on a big rusty nail on the wall in front of me. It seemed to dance while I pulled and pulled, with the heat and smell pressing on my skin and nose, and the cow roaring in anguish. The Grandmother shouted from the kitchen, "Hoory oop, or she'll die under yer hunds— look sharp!"

So I desperately held on to that little foot, pulling it, then losing it, then grasping it again. All of a sudden the mucus gave way and the calf was freed from its mother's belly, sliding out onto the floor.

I stood exhausted. No one spoke, except the young veterinarian who shook my hand and patted my back while I trembled with relief and a shudder went through me, a sudden inexplicable moment of joy.

This was, and has remained, one of the more significant moments of my life.

An Affinity for Trouble

It was in the top drawer of my uncle's dresser that fascinated me. It held decks of Bicycle playing cards, pairs of green dice, and a red Claxton fruitcake tin full of photographs that a boy could not resist. The cards and dice were remnants of his checkered past as a professional gambler, mementos of a career cut short by the law, but it was the fruitcake tin that drew me secretly to his bedroom in the back of my grandmother's house to rummage through his memories.

My uncle never spoke much about his past, his service as a soldier in World War II in the Philippines, his divorce, or his gambling; neither did my parents, who, like most adults in the 1950s, knew more than they were willing to tell. This, of course, made all things adult alluring and forced me into a life of curiosity, occasional deception, and situational ethics, meaning I could break their rules whenever necessary. Occasionally I got away with it. At age twelve, I calculated that I was too old to be spanked, so I adopted the attitude that it was always easier to apologize than to ask permission. And, if you were lucky enough to be tempted to do things that no one had warned you *NOT* to do – e.g., opening my uncle's dresser drawer – the possibilities were limitless.

My uncle was Mother's brother, the eldest of four children. He died in 1973, barely 61 years old. After years of smoking cigarettes, a habit he never tried to quit, saying, "It's the only real pleasure I have left," he finally suffocated from emphysema and congestive heart failure. During the last years of his life, he could not walk 20 paces without stopping to catch his breath.

He was named Francis, after his father, and so the family called him Frank to avoid confusion. But there the similarities ended. My grandfather, who died of a heart attack when I was five years old, was a bailiff who worked in the Jefferson County courthouse in Birmingham and led a sober, quiet middle-class life. I remember him as tall, heavy, and jovial. My uncle was also tall, but slender. He had an angular face, punctuated by a Roman nose, and a sardonic grin that mirrored his world view. He was a hard drinker, a gambler, a fastidious dresser, and never kept a steady job. To most of the family, his faults were appalling, but I felt an affinity with him. Besides, he had attributes that easily offset his character defects.

Frank was of that generation of men who knew how to do things with their hands, useful, necessary, sometimes dangerous things, but always interesting things. He was a skilled do-it-yourself carpenter. He could drive a finishing nail flush with the surface of a board with one strike of a hammer; he was his own auto mechanic and once worked as an aircraft electrician; he collected hand tools of every size and function; and best of all, he occasionally asked me to accompany him to "sight-in" the latest firearm he had acquired.

Frank's disreputable behavior, especially his fondness for drink, distressed his non-drinking parents, yet they stoically endured his frequent binges, which followed a familiar pattern. About once a month, Frank would leave the house and return days later with a roll of bills in his pocket as big as a baseball and a car full of booze. He would stay drunk at the house as long as the money and alcohol lasted.

On hot summer days he could be found on the front porch, in his underwear, drinking and rocking in the old metal glider. He wore dress shoes but left them untied. Socks were optional. He bathed and shaved daily, as though dressing for the office. Mercifully, he stayed hidden from passersby behind a bulwark of gardenias and blue hydrangeas.

He was an amiable drunk, never violent or mean-spirited, and generous, which always attracted a crowd of relatives. He once gave my brother a $100 bill to retrieve his car from a downtown parking lot. My brother was about to pocket the windfall when our mother saw what was going on and demanded that he return the money. My brother still laments, "If only she had walked into the room three seconds later."

I was luckier. He gave me a $20 bill, more money than I had ever seen, and I spent all of it on a radio-controlled model airplane before my mother could find out. It had a 36-inch wingspan and took weeks to build. To my surprise Mother never said anything, even after learning I had crashed my treasure on its maiden flight.

My parents, and my cousin Jimmy's, tried to limit our exposure to Frank. On one occasion when we wanted to visit him, Jimmy's mother demurred, saying, "Uncle Frank isn't feeling well," which prompted Jimmy to reply: "But that's why we want to go see him."

Sadly for my cousin and me, Frank's gambling career came to a sudden end one day, although it wasn't until I was grown that I learned the details. My father, who found humor in his brother-in-law's adventures, explained: "I went out to the front yard one morning to get the paper, and when I opened it to the front page, there was Frank, handcuffed with a deputy sheriff at each elbow." The arrest had followed a raid at one of my uncle's gambling hangouts. The accompanying news story disclosed that Frank had pleaded with the deputies not to arrest him, because he was the sole support of his invalid mother. That was news to the family, however. My grandmother, the head dietitian at the local grammar school, was actually my uncle's sole support.

With gambling gone, my uncle eventually quit drinking, although I don't recall the time frame. He never explained it. The only reminder of his front-porch days was a missing upper incisor, which he had yanked out with pliers during a binge. A toothache, he reasoned, wasn't worth the cost of a dentist; he could do it himself. "Dentistry's nothing but a high-class trade," he said.

My uncle still went out most nights, though no one knew where. He usually wore one of his pinstriped Hickey Freeman suits and always returned in time to watch the ten o'clock news. There was never another run-in with the sheriff. Or another binge. Frank lived peacefully except for the occasional flare-up over the civil rights movement. He was vociferous in his defense of segregation, as Birmingham became the nation's billboard for racism in the 1960s. We would argue about it from time to time. I took the side of

civil rights, he the side of George Wallace, whose dema-
goguery, "I say segregation now, segregation tomorrow,
segregation forever," had gotten him elected governor. He
listened to my viewpoint, even if he did shrug it off: "It
must be something they're teaching in school," which, in
Birmingham in 1962, was about as likely as the Hitler Youth
helping elderly Jews to cross the street. Teachers at my all-
white high school never addressed the issue of race. I learned
my views by witnessing the ugly reality of segregation around
me and from the clergy at my Episcopal church, who taught
that Jesus' commandment to "love one another" meant
everybody. There was no loophole allowing "White Only"
and "Colored" water fountains.

By the Sixties, my uncle's hair was thin and silver. He
wore it in a close-cropped flattop that made his receding
hairline less noticeable. His face was virtually unwrinkled. As
he aged, he developed a germ phobia, the result of his attempt
to prevent a stray upper respiratory infection from attacking
his defenseless lungs. He routinely bade visitors to dip their
hands in the large bowl of Lysol he placed on the table by the
front door. He never touched a doorknob or the TV without
shielding his fingers with a Kleenex. In those years, he spent
much of his generous allotment of free time inert in a recliner
from which he greeted guests without rising. "Pardon my
laziness," he would drawl, extending his right hand and
revealing his gap-toothed smile.

It was from this perch that he also dispensed
unsolicited advice that was almost always given after you had
screwed up. "It looks like you would have known that
beforehand," was his inevitable opening line. Only once do I
recall his advising me on the front end. He urged me to marry
the girl I was dating because her family had money, and,

further, to get her pregnant to insure my place in their hearts and my financial future. Fortunately for all concerned, that never happened.

He was not blind to his own faults, though, declaring to me once in a surprising flash of insight, "I've been a damn fool most of my life," but it was in his observations of the foibles of others that he truly excelled. Of two female family members, who habitually visited their doctors for "nerve medicine," he cracked, "If I was a doctor, Darla and Helen would be the only patients I'd ever need."

One of the last times I saw Frank was days before I entered the military. I was close to flunking out of college, facing the draft and a sure ticket to Vietnam. I joined the Coast Guard in 1966, believing the recruiter when he said only volunteers go to Southeast Asia. I wanted to share the news with my uncle, who was in the VA hospital being treated for his emphysema. As I entered his room, he bummed a cigarette from me and disappeared into the bathroom to smoke it. I heard the toilet flush, and he emerged, with not a shred of irony on his face. I related my plans. He looked at me and grinned, "Heh, heh, you'll see, you'll see just what kind of shit you got yourself into."

I think that's why he rarely talked about his war. A draftee, he had been through the shit and didn't want to relive it. I asked him once what he did in the war, and he only laughed, "I set up casinos on the rec deck." Yet he was a hero to me. He had fought the Japanese, surviving three years of island-hopping combat in the Pacific. I don't know if he had nightmares or regrets, but I do know he admired the Japanese in some ways, a view I have always assumed he formed during his time stationed in Japan after the surrender. I never heard him speak of them as the enemy.

It was a contradiction, as was much of his life. Despite his wild ways, his bigotry, bluster, cynicism, and his chiseling, he loved his family, including me. As an adolescent trying to avoid my parents' alcohol-fueled quarrels, I felt secure in his sober presence. Visits to my grandmother's house grew more frequent after I started driving. It was my haven where I was always welcomed and loved unconditionally, a place with no drinking and no fighting.

I was still welcome there after I started my own drinking in high school. Frank knew what I was doing even if my grandmother didn't. Only once did he say anything. I was due to help him work on a carpentry project at the house, and I arrived late and severely hung over after a big Saturday night party. He put me to work right away. I was assigned the task of squaring the ends of several two-by-fours with a handsaw, a skill at which my uncle was a master. It was hot, and I was sweating. My head was pounding, and I couldn't saw a straight line with my shaking hand. "How much did you drink last night?" he demanded. When I weakly replied, "A couple of beers," he growled, "Boy, I bet if you pissed in a jar right now you'd fill it with Budweiser. You're trying to kid the kidder."

I don't think he ever knew I snooped through his dresser drawer. I know I never asked him about the photographs. There must have been a hundred in that fruitcake tin: pictures of Japanese gardens and Shinto shrines; others of smiling army buddies; many I don't remember. But there is one, still vivid in my memory, if others blur. It is a snapshot of a group of GIs, standing in a jungle clearing, arms around each other's shoulders. They are smiling. At their feet, on a bed of palm leaves, rest the heads of six or seven Japanese soldiers who had been executed. Their eyes are

closed, faces oddly at peace. One of the GIs is holding a
Samurai sword at his side. Frank is not in the picture.

I do not know what happened to the photos after
Frank died. I was living in Florida then, working for a
newspaper. When the news of his death came, too late for
me to attend his funeral, I got drunk, which was becoming
routine. I had not thought about those photographs in years
and did not think of them that day. I thought of my uncle,
though, and took another drink. Frank's war was over while
mine was beginning, although I did not know it then. I was
still trying to kid the kidder.

Too Bright

On a midsummer evening when the afterglow of the western sky lasted until ten, my parents, Peggy and Dicky, stepped out for a while gently closing their apartment door so as not to wake me. They strolled along Mansfield Avenue away from the Yale campus for cherished time together—Dicky had left that morning at seven. During the two hours since he arrived home their energetic one year-old had worn herself out and them too. Their walk was to be a restorative.

On returning, my parents found me on the dresser top smeared with something red. Rushing over, they saw that it was blood, but were relieved that I had only minor cuts. Much later, I heard my father recount the incident: Gretchen climbed out of her crib, pulled on the two dresser drawers just enough to get a toehold and scrambled to the top where the alarm clock sat.

Each evening my father wound the clock while putting me to bed. In the mornings, its clang alerted me to the first enchantment of the day, watching as my father and my mother slowly came to life. On my own that night, I was intent on making the magic happen. Instead, I broke the glass and pulled off the hour and minute hands.

My parents marveled that though bloody, I was not crying and appeared utterly absorbed in tinkering. No barrier would hold me back; I had walked at about ten months. Alarmed, relieved, and chastened about their absence, they nonetheless conveyed wonder at their Little Gretchen.

Another story I heard my father tell was about a fixation of mine that was possibly injurious.

"Gretchen would bang her head on the floor," he chortled, not seeing it as harmful. In my life I have known smart women who were head bangers in childhood and sure enough it didn't damage them in any lasting fashion. Dicky used me as an example when friends asked his advice about their kids' untamed behavior.

My maternal grandmother, with whom I spent a month at age six, recalled other behavior. She wrote my parents:

> Gretchen seems perfectly happy, but
> extremely nervous and I think entirely too
> bright for her years. I am glad, Dick, you are
> a sociologist, because maybe you can do
> something to tame her, but if she isn't tamed
> I am afraid she will break wide open some
> day, and that before her time.

Curious, precocious, bright, but a menace to herself is the "me" of childhood, according to my parents and one grandmother. By the time I could think about such things, I had my own ideas.

As a high school girl in the 1950s, I had a lot to rage about: the unfairness of southern society, classmates' conformity, social cliques, and bullies. My friend Jack teased me, said that I had a "satchel butt" and sometimes grabbed me there. My sociologist father was no help. He maintained that boys teased me because they liked me, teasing was their way of showing it. My mother agreed.

Girls who were going steady had their protectors, but the wolves saw me as bait. My tendency to act hysterical when calling out a bully would goad him to greater dares. So I began putting on a serious demeanor as my protection.

I became a harder working student by challenging myself in Latin and subjects which then were associated with male intelligence—advanced Algebra, Solid Geometry, and Trigonometry. Under the influence of my father, who knew a lot about physical science, I decided to take Physics. That would subdue the kidders, I presumed.

My Physics classmates included guys who wanted to become engineers, physicians, military pilots, and photographers and a few girls with broad horizons. The jocks and their fawning girlfriends were not there, nor was my brainy best friend Jensene, who took over as editor of the yearbook when her cousin Walter, a jock, failed to put in enough time to get the work done.

The science classroom with its tall ceiling, long rows of elevated lab counters, high metal chairs, and soaring windows connoted lofty matters. Glass-fronted cases held all sorts of paraphernalia, like balances, measuring gadgets, specimens of minerals, fossils, and for biology class, stuffed birds, snakes, and fishes. But near the windows I could watch a wider world, catch fresh air, and see green expanses, live oak trees, and cars passing in the distance on US 441. Daydream sometimes.

In the warm afternoons, managing the huge windows and their linen shades fell to the guys. The chosen one pulled the cords to close the bottom shade and open the upper one. He then grabbed the wooden staff and mated its metal hook with the eye socket on the upper sash. I liked this masculine display. Each guy did it differently; rippling his muscles, heaving and pulling the sash down while the hidden window-chain clanked inside its casing. The western breeze moved the shades slowly forward and backward; a gust startled the wooden baffle at the bottom. At its clatter, fresh air rushed in. That classroom itself was a lesson in thermal drafts and temperature.

From tall, pale Mr. Pate, despite his unanimated delivery, I learned useful subject matter. He described and demonstrated the internal combustion engine so vividly that I, a newly licensed driver, could admire the logic and usefulness of our family-car's engine. When my father was teaching me to drive he pointed out the features under the hood and how to check the oil. The few times I witnessed an engine that had boiled over I was astonished at the hissing steam that could peel paint and the boiling water and hot metal that would scar a man for life. Mr. Pate's lessons helped me much later to understand my husband's natter about two-stroke bikes, V-8 engines, overhead cams, and misfiring, which I associated with chocking acrid smoke. I still had a fascination for how things worked.

One afternoon, almost late, I bopped up the left aisle to my space on the second row nearest the window at a two-person elevated counter with a lab sink in the middle. I heaved my books and purse onto this surface. Joe, a six-footer who sat directly behind me, was fiddling with the twine of the shades and bullshitting with another guy. Stepping aside, he positioned

himself behind my chair with his hands resting on the top
—the signal of a gentleman who would pull out the lady's
chair. "Thank you," I said, bending to sit. Joe yanked the chair
away. I fell far and hit hard. Screaming, I snatched his arm and
bit down viciously.

Running from the room in hysterics, I surged through
the deserted halls. Needing a tranquil place with someone to
comfort me, I avoided the busy school office. Instinct turned
me to the corridor of the primary school toward the school
nurse's office. Bursting in, through heaving sobs I blurted out
to Mrs. Buchannan what had happened in the classroom with
Joe and my mortification at biting him. In her pithy way she
calmed me down, led me behind a curtain to a darkened cubicle
with a cot, and handed me a box of Kleenex. I wiped my eyes,
blew my nose, pulled off my loafers, and crawled under the
spread. My well-padded butt barely hurt, but my dignity was
bruised. In this sanctuary I slept.

Later I heard subdued tones—Mr. Pate had arrived
and was talking with the nurse. He shambled into the cubicle,
with my books and purse that I had left in class, and took a
seat. Speaking in the same low tone, he expressed regret about
the incident in his classroom and his inattention while
preparing materials for the lecture. He let me know that he
spoke to the class about the need for more mature conduct
and with Joe about his insensitive prank. Soon the principal
sent word to the nurse who telephoned Mother that I could
go home for the rest of the day.

The next day when I arrived at Physics, Joe apologized,
and I accepted. Joe was easy going, a cut-up, but smart; I
relaxed again in his presence.

Months later Joe took me to the post-graduation party, not
really a date. Before we left my father took photos of us

clowning—Joe with his graduation tassel swinging from his ear and me grimacing in surprise. We headed to the rustic lake house outside town belonging to a classmate's family. At the house we dug into a spread of fried chicken, potato salad, and watermelon, and bottles of Coke, Nehi, and Dr. Pepper from a tin tub of ice. The dancing began in earnest for couples, while others of us changed and headed for the water. Joe hung out at the house yakking with some other guys headed for military service.

I waded into the water from the sandy approach toward other girls. I was christening my white pique' one-piece suit, but was apprehensive. As I swam and lolled on that balmy starlit night, I kept looking down to see if my nipples showed through the wet suit, but the light from the dock was dim. Wafting from the house were amorous lyrics such as Patti Page's, "Do you remember the night of the Tennessee Waltz when ..." and Rosemary Clooney's "Come on-a my house, my house come on." No romance for us swimmers, just guys doing belly flops off the dock to splash our hair while the chaperones darted back and forth from us to the house, where couples might be going too far.

In a flash Jack, Julian, and Vance moved in on and surrounded me.

"What are you doing?" I asked, hoping it was a watery square dance. Then one of them grabbed my arm and tugged me across and beyond the sandy bottom into a place of muck, reeds, and grasses. I feared stepping on something that would cut me or a slithery creature that might bite me. Then the circle reformed with me in the middle. Breathless and nervous, I started yelling at them, still thinking they were little kids at a prank.

"Let me go. Quit. Dammit." Though a good swimmer, I was no match for three guys. They had towed me beyond the party site to shallower water where it was not deep enough to do more than wade. I squirmed to elude them and when I did, one caught me and I slipped into the muck. I ducked below the water surface but could not get beyond their legs and reemerged. My white suit smudged.

"You bastards leave me alone," and then directing my cries toward the dock and house, "Help!"

One grabbed my suit strap, another, the back. They were trying to peel it off. I screamed louder. I struggled as one wrapped his arms around me from the back. In a moment of hush, I heard swishing of water. I detected a tall figure with wide shoulders at a distance striding through the reeds.

"Who else is joining this melee?" I silently wondered if God was even aware of my distress. Would I be stripped and grabbed? A humiliation loomed for me, or maybe worse.

Drawing closer, I recognized the figure as Mr. Gibson, our homeroom teacher. He kept coming and I knew this to be a miracle. I would be rescued. The boys recognized him too. In a beat, they had released me, resuming nonchalant poses. He came into the middle of the clutch and sternly ordered them back to the dock.

As Mr. Pate months before, Mr. Gibson comforted me and rebuked the bullies. I trusted these male teachers like I did my father. Men came in different temperaments, and I was learning for my future in a man's world.

When I found my grandmother's letter after half a century, I wanted to cry. She saw the threat to a happy, too bright girl coming in contact with a world that would bruise her. She herself, as a young widow, had forged a path which demanded pluck and courage to support herself and her child, my mother, Peggy.

I guess what my grandmother predicted had come to pass—that I *would* break wide open. As far as her idea that I would need to be tamed, well ... maybe—though as far as I was concerned, the brutes, the bigots, and sociopaths were ones who needed to be caged.

Swimming

When I was a freshman at Georgia Tech in 1961, I dreaded taking a required phys-ed course called PT 101-Swimming. Its creator and instructor was Fred Lanoue, the head coach of Tech's swimming team. He was widely known to be both crotchety and demanding. And his course had a fearsome reputation. Some upperclassmen who'd been through it thought it might be better named PT 101-Drowning.

Along with twenty-five other innocents, I filed into the bleachers beside Georgia Tech's indoor pool, and took a seat. Coach Lanoue climbed out of the water and toweled himself off. Grabbing his clipboard, he called the roll. I sized him up. He couldn't have been more than five-feet-two, and he looked old enough to be my grandfather. He was bald, skinny and shrunken. A misshapen leg hung from his left hip. He didn't so much walk, as he sidled. And he had on only the briefest of swimsuits, one I would have been embarrassed to wear.

Though his appearance was not impressive, his voice was. He spoke with a kind of gruff bark, with great authority, like a drill sergeant lecturing a bunch of new recruits. "This is a swimming class," he growled, "but I'm *not* here to teach you how to swim. You should know that already. If you don't, it's too late for me to do much about it." A not-so-great swimmer myself, I wondered what any non-swimmers must be thinking. He went on. "What I *am* here to do is teach you how *not* to drown. Listen carefully, do exactly what I tell you, and you'll never, ever be in danger of dying in deep water."

Coach Lanoue's method for not drowning was called drown-proofing. We spent weeks learning it. Its principles—as the coach described them—were simple. "Take a deep breath and assume the position of the dead man's float, your head, arms and legs hanging down in the water. Every twenty seconds or so, bring your head up and refill your lungs, expending as little energy as possible as you tread the water with your arms and legs. Resume the dead-man position." It was Coach Lanoue's contention that by establishing a steady rhythm of these moves, anyone could stay afloat for hours.

Much as I tried, I couldn't master the pace that drown-proofing required. Some days I might be able to sustain it for fifteen minutes. Others, I'd have to swim, gurgling and flailing, to the side of the pool, after five. Coach Lanoue had little patience with slow learners like me. His idea of poolside assistance was a damning curse accompanied by a push on your head with his bad leg.

As we approached the time for the first test of our drown-proofing prowess, Coach Lanoue described what we'd be doing. "Take this piece of rope. Cross your ankles and tie them together with one end. Loop the other end around your waist and tie it back to itself at your navel. Crawl to the edge of the pool and push yourself in. Use drown-proofing to stay afloat for twenty minutes. I'll time you. Go to the bottom. Retrieve this plastic ring you'll find there. After that, use drown-proofing and your arms to swim your way across the width of the pool—two times. Do all that, and I'll give you an 'A.' Anything less and I'll decide how much credit I think you deserve."

Was he serious?

Damn right he was!

Test day came, and the best I could manage was the twenty minute float and one side-to-side swim. I was surprised that I could do even that. Amazingly, half the class did it all.

The tests that followed weren't any easier. We had to perform similarly challenging feats with our hands tied behind our backs, and then with both our hands and feet tied. I muddled through with minimal credit. Was I going to pass this course, or would I end up having to take it again? It was required in order to graduate. I feared I might end up like a senior in the class who told me that he had failed the course twice already, and that his ability to earn his degree was in serious jeopardy.

It was a relief to be finished with drown-proofing. The test that followed was more to my liking. Jump from the high platform with your clothes on. Take off your pants, knot the legs, and inflate them into a makeshift life preserver. Use it to stay afloat for fifteen minutes. I'd done this in Boy Scouts. I did it again for the test. Things were looking up.

Coach Lanoue described our final challenge—a 50-yard swim, two lengths of the pool, down and back, from a diving start. There would be two wrinkles. The first: We'd have to stay underwater for the entire swim. The second: Just to be sure that the diving start didn't give anyone an advantage, we'd have to do an underwater flip immediately after we'd dived. Coach said the whole test should take each of us about a minute.

Even some of the good swimmers in the class seemed concerned. Fifty yards underwater was a long way. One minute without a breath could seem an eternity. Coach Lanoue was sure that everyone could do it. And again, he had a method. If we just did what he was going to teach us, there was no way we could fail. "Just like drown-proofing," I was thinking.

Part 1 of Coach Lanoue's method: "Before you dive, hyperventilate. For about a minute, take deep breaths in rapid succession. Make each exhale as long and forceful as you can. Inhale naturally after each exhale. When your fingers begin to tingle, you're ready to dive."

Part 2: "Take long, smooth, steady strokes with your arms, and make frog-like kicks with your legs. Glide. Relax. There's no rush. There's plenty of oxygen in your lungs. When you reach the far end of the pool, turn and push off with a good kick. Glide and stroke some more. You'll be back to where you started before you know it."

I practiced this swim diligently for two weeks. I practiced it during classes, and I practiced it between classes. I must have gone through twenty rehearsals. Breathing, diving, flipping, stroking, kicking, turning, gliding—I polished all my moves. But during none of this practice was I ever able to make it further than about thirty of the required fifty yards. An undeniable need for air would take hold, and I'd have to surface.

Test day arrived. We sat in the bleachers waiting our turn to be called. Coach Lanoue prefaced the session with new information. It was possible, he said, that some of us might pass-out mid-swim during this test. Not to worry. The body's natural reaction, when this took place, would be to prevent water from coming into the lungs. If he saw it happen to anyone, he'd have them brought out of the water, and they'd get an automatic A. I wanted no part of that outcome.

As the first swimmer took his dive and made his flip, Coach Lanoue droned. "Those of you who think this guy might need help are welcome to begin the first verse of 'Onward Christian Soldiers.'" A few who apparently appreciated the irony started singing. But most of us, including me, just stared … with growing wonder. The brave soul we were watching made a clean turn, stroked smoothly through his final lap and emerged arms-raised at the finish. Cheers rang-out across the pool, and echoed off the walls. It was indeed possible to complete this test.

Even more incredibly, the next five swimmers succeeded. Coach Lanoue shouted their times as they touched the finish. Each one was within ten seconds of the sixty the coach had told us we would need. The class was on a roll. I was becoming a believer. But would I be the one to break our string?

A classmate we all knew to be a poor swimmer nervously took his place at poolside. He hyperventilated and dove. His flip left him pointed in the wrong direction. A few tentative strokes took him into the side wall. He bounced off and headed back to where he'd started. Another ten seconds of going nowhere, and he'd had enough. He surfaced, dog-paddled to a ladder and climbed out. Coach Lanoue muttered an unintelligible curse. "Thank God," I thought. "I won't be the first."

Then Coach Lanoue's prediction came true. An accomplished swimmer, I'll call him Joe, stretched his arms forward five yards from the finish. His body froze. The coach watched intently—as did we all—for about five seconds.

Coach signaled an assistant who was standing poolside to go down and bring Joe up. In his rescuer's clutches and gasping for air, Joe looked blankly in our direction, as if he'd just been waked from a crazy dream. Later he told us that he didn't remember anything beyond his dive. Coach had called it. Joe had no water in his lungs. And he'd earned his "A."

By the time my turn came, I had seen it all—success, failure, even brief unconsciousness. I stood at the end of the pool. Exhaling and inhaling, with extreme emphasis—as Coach Lanoue had stressed—on the exhales, I felt the ends of my fingers tingle. It was time. I dove.

I vaguely remember turning my flip and taking a couple of strokes. My next recollection is of touching a wall and kicking back toward where I'd come from. Though I saw the break in the pool bottom where shallow water began tapering down to deep, the last five yards beyond it didn't register. I touched the finishing wall and heard the coach's voice, "63 seconds." And ... clapping hands!

A prouder moment I'd never known. I'd aced the test and passed the course. And I'd done it with a feat that sounded impossible when I'd first heard Coach Lanoue describe it, a feat I'd not been able to do in practice, a feat I'd surely never have to do again.

To my great surprise, I was saddened to hear that Coach Fred Lanoue had died unexpectedly, in 1963, the year before I graduated. Though still in his sixties, he'd suffered a massive heart attack while drown-proofing Marines at Parris Island, South Carolina. His legacy, however, was to live on for decades, in stories like mine that his students still tell, and in a book he wrote about drown-proofing. And his drown-proofing techniques would continue to be used for training by the military, the State Department and the Peace Corps. Despite his didacticism and orneriness, many of us Tech grads will never forget his incredible class and the seemingly miraculous accomplishments he gave us the knowledge and the courage to complete.

A Reluctant Evangelist

I flirted with fundamentalism during my college years. I'd met a group of charismatic Christian students, who talked about their faith with the same zeal a weight lifter, beefed up on steroids and vanity, promotes his health regimen. They claimed to be "on fire for Christ" and spoke in terms of "saved" and "damned." The Rapture was their focus, and they feared Satan crept around every corner.

It was a far cry from the faith of the potlucking, blue-haired church ladies, who smelled like a sachet of gardenias and mothballs, and shushed me every Sunday morning during my father's sermon. Those women taught me the stories of Jesus, using flannel boards and felt cutouts of Bible characters, and they could sing most hymns without ever looking down at a hymnal. They spent their spare time delivering meals to shut-ins and collecting winter coats for the poor. And even though they'd lived through the Depression and sent their husbands and sons off to war, there was always hope in their eyes. They saw goodness in every person they met.

But this new group of Christians was different. They were a part of the phenomenon known as the "Toronto Blessing." And when the Holy Spirit descended upon them, they'd crawl around on all fours barking like dogs and roaring like lions. At times they even spoke in tongues.

Not everyone was blessed with the Spirit, they'd say. It was a gift reserved for the most faithful, though if you were desperate enough they'd beat your chest until the Spirit filled your heart and loosened your tongue. Then you, too, could speak in the language of angels. "Glossolalia" it is called, and it was the mark of the inner circle. I remember thinking that anyone would start speaking gibberish if they were beaten long enough, just to make it stop. Yet every night I'd lay awake wondering why it was I'd never spoken in tongues. I didn't want to bark like a dog or roar like a lion. I was petrified of losing my senses. But I longed for intimacy, and I couldn't help wondering why Christ didn't want to be as close to me as he apparently was to them. What was wrong with me?

Pastor Mike and his followers were always quick with an answer to this question: I lacked faith. What's more, I'd been baptized as an infant and couldn't point to the exact moment I accepted Christ as my Savior. I even liked kissing my boyfriend. And if that wasn't enough, I never spoke out against the people God hated most: the feminists, the atheists, the secularists, and most especially the homosexuals. We were all destined for hell.

They'd read Christ's commandment to go into the world and make disciples and understood it literally. The proof of their love of Christ was found in the number of souls they converted, and on Friday nights they'd head into town.

"If you were to die this very night, do you know where your soul would go?" they'd cry out to a couple walking hand in hand on their way into a movie theater. Or they'd sidle up next to a man waiting for a bus while immersed in a good novel, tap him on the shoulder and ask, "If Christ met you at the gates of Heaven and asked why He should let you in, what would you say?"

Brash, fearless, and aggressive, they were veritable Custers in the war for souls. By the end of every campaign, all of their captives—hardened and flagrant sinners as they were—had repented, had invited Christ into their hearts, and had become bona fide Christians, heaven bound.

Celebrations ensued with a bottle of soda, a pizza, and a rousing game of Pictionary. These Christians knew how to have a good time, but the fun was lost on me. All I could think about was how much I wanted to follow that couple into the House of Sin, as they called it, and sit in the dark with a bucket of popcorn and watch a movie, any movie, or get my hands on the novel that poor man at the bus stop was reading, even though my friends would tell me to burn it if they caught sight of it, because it wasn't written by a Christian, and made no mention of Christ or salvation or hell.

When it came to sharing my faith, I took a General McClellan approach. I'd find a woman sitting on a park bench or in a coffee shop, sit down next to her and compliment her on her shoes. We'd talk about the weather and where we grew up. I'd ask what she did for a living and eventually slip in a reference to Jesus. But I was always quick to retreat at the first sign of impending failure. The slightest curling of a lip or furrowing of a brow would send me running.

I was terrified that Christ would return and discover I had converted no souls. In desperation I devised a plan. I went down to the Christian bookstore and found 3x5 glossy tracts written especially for the stalwart Christian out to make disciples. Unusually ambitious, I bought a stack of one hundred. That night, armed with my Bible, a journal and a handful of my newly purchased tracts, I went to the Black-eyed Pea for dinner.

Nestling myself into a corner table by a window, I opened my Bible and began reading, careful to appear as though I found every word to be thoroughly poignant and revelatory. When the waitress came, I looked up at her with large, discerning eyes and smiled softly, hoping my gentle nature might woo her into conversation. My effort was lost upon her. She didn't even make eye contact when she asked what I'd like to drink. Instead, she looked to the door at the crowds pouring in.

I took this as a cue not to waste her time, ordered a glass of ice water and a cheeseburger with mustard, and went back to reading the Scriptures. She returned shortly afterward and slid across the table a tepid glass of water and a cheeseburger dripping with mayonnaise. I feel towards mayonnaise the way most people feel about looking at a flesh wound. But I ate it anyway, knowing that refusing to do so could have eternal consequences.

When the bill came I shoved some cash into the vinyl holder and retreated to my car to watch as the waitress opened what was really more of a Trojan horse of sorts, as I had sandwiched in between the bills a tract I had handpicked for the waitress's presumably lost soul. I wasn't sure what would happen next; whether she'd shake her clinched fists at the air and curse my existence or, even worse, point me out to the manager and have me banned for life. I was more than relieved when she scanned the tract, flipped it over a couple of times, and stuffed it into her apron pocket. I regarded this as an overwhelming success and considered the waitress the first soul I ever led to Christ.

I repeated this exact pattern dozens of times, the only deviation being that I started leaving a heftier tip, thinking it might soften the blow a weighted conscience was sure to feel upon the realization of her depravity. Each waitress who did not wad up the tract and toss it to the floor, I deemed a victory. I'd head home gratified that I had saved a soul. But by the time I walked through the front door I was full of remorse, because she—like me—now felt the burden of her sin and could never escape it, no matter how hard she tried.

Good Golly, Aunt Lolly

A good Christian woman. That's how everyone at Aunt Lolly's funeral described her. "That she was, but she took that shit a little too far," I muttered, as the guilt of my black thoughts grabbed me by the throat.

"Look at my pretty red shoes," she'd once said to ten-year-old me. "Don't they remind you of the blood of Jesus? You know, He shed His blood on the cross to redeem us of our sins." "Yes, those are nice shoes, Aunt Lolly," I replied, realizing the oddness of her analogy even in my guileless mind. She was never one to miss an opportunity to witness to those whose salvation might be in question.

Aunt Lolly was my maternal grandmother's oldest sister, the firstborn of the nine Sanders children. Aunt Lolly's twin sister, Molly, had died at birth; a topic I never heard her discuss, though she would readily boast of her four brothers who served in World War II, and all came back alive.

She dutifully carried the burden of Methodist piety, with expectations that her siblings were following suit. Shorter in stature than most of her family, she kept her weight under control, and was quick to point out those who did not. "You really should try to reduce," she'd advise her portly sisters. The harsh cat-eye glasses of her younger days eventually gave way to huge round lenses that swallowed her face, and then softened to gold wire bifocals when she reached her twilight years. Her white hair, brushed back from her forehead, fell in soft waves that stopped at her nape. Red nail polish did little to disguise evidence of her lifetime of hard work.

As with most daughters of the Depression-era South, she left school before graduating, to help her farmer father, and spent her teen years toiling with her sisters in a Coweta County, Georgia, hosiery mill, that was devoid of both air conditioning and labor laws. She married in her twenties, a fellow mill worker, Roy Shellnut, her 'til-death-do-us-part husband, and she bore him three sons. Oddly, Roy was also a twin—Lolly and Molly and Roy and Ray. They left mill work to raise hogs on acreage they bought in a community called Goodes (it rhymes with "foods").

"Let's ride out to Goodes to see Lolly and Roy," Grandmommie Frieda would say.

"Goodes?" I asked. "What in the world is a Goode?"

"Why, that's where your Aunt Lolly lives," she answered as I shrugged my shoulders and hopped into her silver Ford.

I later learned that many areas of unincorporated Georgia were named by and for the folks who first settled there, and I was relieved that the misfortune of a last name like "Goode" had eluded me.

Aunt Lolly lived in a charming 1930s brick, English Tudor house with an arched front door, and an arched screened porch on its side. Inside were built-in nooks, shelves and cabinets. They were filled with knickknacks—figurines of birds and children, and colored glass vases. "Don't touch," Grandmommie reminded. I wished that my house had nooks where I could sit my ceramic tiger bank and miniature doll with yellow hair that smelled of lemons.

Uncle Roy was a jovial little man who made us feel welcome, and freely dished out candy to tiny open palms. He wore the waist of his pants nearly under his armpits, giving his body a funhouse mirror look. When he wasn't talking, he was whistling, and if you visited near Christmas, he'd sing a little jingle:

"Oooooh, boy. Santa Claus is coming. Sack of oranges. Sack of apples. Oooooh, boy."

"Oranges? Apples? I sure hope not," I thought. "I'm holding out for a Malibu Barbie."

I suppose if you asked anyone in my family what they remember most about Aunt Lolly, it would be her strawberry cake. We counted on having that pink goodness at every family gathering. "That cake's made entirely from scratch," she would brag. "No sir, you won't find a cake mix in my house."

"He who hesitates is lost," my Uncle Jack would say as he grabbed the last slice, grinning at the defeated cousin who had waited a bit too long to let his dinner settle. "I should have made two," Aunt Lolly would reply. But, she never did. She knew to keep us begging for more.

The weeks I spent with Grandmommie Frieda each summer were chock-full of visits with her sisters, Mildred and Lolly. Laughter is what I remember most of those visits. The three of them chatting, with me silently observing from an antique wooden milking stool in the corner of my grandmother's overfilled living room. Reminiscing, gossiping, joking, and usually ending with the revelation of a perfect man Mildred or Lolly had spied for my widowed grandmother.

"Oh, good Lord, Lolly!" Grandmommie would scowl. "What in the world do I need with a man?" Then she'd tell them about Mr. Taylor asking her to join him for lunch at the Shrimp Boat after church last Sunday.

"Well, well," the sisters would say, grinning.

"Oh, for gosh sakes! It was just lunch," she'd snap. I haven't got any use for an old man."

After Aunt Mildred passed away, the sisterly bond between Grandmommie Frieda and Aunt Lolly tightened. "Frieda, grab ya pocketbook and paint ya lips. We're goin' to lunch at Sprague's Barbeque. I'll pick ya up in a jiffy," Aunt Lolly barked into the phone receiver. And, there they'd sit, grieving for Mildred over pulled pork and Brunswick stew.

My uncle, Jack, accompanied them to Sprague's Barbeque on one occasion. At the end of the meal, Aunt Lolly grabbed the check and paid the waitress. As they headed to the car, Aunt Lolly said, "Well, thank y'all for taking me out, but you really should've let me pay the tab." "But, you did pay, Aunt Lolly," Uncle Jack reminded her. "Oh, did I?" she asked. "Well, I guess I'm gettin' right forgetful," she reasoned. Sadly, that was the beginning of Aunt Lolly's end.

"It wouldn't be Easter without one of your strawberry cakes," my mom's sister, Jessie, told Aunt Lolly when she asked what she could bring to the family gathering. We were all set to celebrate Resurrection Sunday at the newly renovated East Point home of Aunt Jessie and Uncle Don. Their primary residence was in Smyrna, and this was a second home they'd purchased to live in on weekdays while their two children attended nearby Woodward Academy. The home was just off Main Street in a gentrified neighborhood still scary enough to warrant chaining down the porch furniture. They'd transformed it from a ramshackle wreck to a quaint cottage, white picket fence and all.

As the family arrived, Uncle Don gave everyone the "ten-cent-tour," as he called it. We oohed and aahed at the skillful arrangement of antique furniture, brass candlesticks, colorful quilts, and carnival glass. "Just put your casserole dishes on the kitchen island," Aunt Jessie directed. "We're going to serve ourselves buffet style."

Aunt Lolly set down her pedestal cake plate with its shiny domed lid hiding what was awaiting us underneath. It didn't take a clairvoyant to recognize that every family member was secretly plotting their after-dinner strategy for snagging a coveted slice of Aunt Lolly's special confection.

Everyone had their fill of ham and potato salad, and lingered at the table over polite conversation and sweaty iced tea glasses, waiting for Aunt Jessie to announce that dessert was being served. "Come help me pour up the coffee and plate the desserts, Gwen," she directed. I followed her into the kitchen and began lining up the coffee cups.

"What in God's name is this pile of shit?" Aunt Jessie screamed. I turned to see her standing with the cake dome in her hand glaring at a mound of what looked like regurgitated strawberries.

"Oh, no," I said. "Aunt Lolly's losing her mind, for sure."

"How am I supposed to serve this mess?" Aunt Jessie asked. "It looks like coagulated blood."

"Shhh … don't let her hear you," I cautioned. "It'll hurt her feelings."

"She forgot to drain the strawberries," Aunt Jessie surmised.

"Or add the baking powder," I guessed.

"You go out there and whisper a warning to everyone so they won't look shocked when they see it. Tell them to push it around on the plate with their forks, plop their napkins on top, and tell her how good it was," Aunt Jessie schemed.

"Okay," I promised.

One by one, as everyone filed into the kitchen, we stifled our looks of horror as we dished up spoonsful rather than slices of what had been the anticipated highlight of our day. The fork pushing and napkin dropping ensued, and Aunt Lolly beamed as the false accolades rolled in.

"As usual, Lolly, you really knocked it out of the park with that strawberry cake of yours," said Uncle Bennie.

"You have got to give me the recipe, Lolly," said Aunt Darla. "I know mine won't be as delicious as yours, but I've got to give it a try."

"Yep, there's nothing better on this side of heaven than a piece of Aunt Lolly's strawberry cake," my mom added.

Aunt Jessie and I hurriedly took out the trash, removing all evidence of our successful ploy.

The next time I saw Aunt Lolly was at Grandmommie Frieda's funeral in 1994. The thief called "dementia" had not yet stolen Lolly's red nails, coiffed hair, or Sunday dress. Though she pretended to know me, her vacant look gave her away.

The details of my grandmother's funeral service are hazy now. My mind checked out during Uncle Jack's solo of "It Is Well with My Soul," Grandmommie's favorite song. Mentally running from the painfulness of permanent goodbyes, I had distracted myself with the sound of Aunt Lolly's occasional whimpers, and wondered if people with dementia still feel grief, or if they just mimic the behavior of those around them.

After the burial, the family gathered at Grandmommie Frieda's house and shared a meal prepared by good Southern Baptist friends and longtime neighbors. My cousin, Susan, decided that a six-pack of Coors Light was what she needed to diminish her grief. Uncle Jack, a Protestant minister at the time, met her at the door. "We'll have none of that in my mother's house," he told Susan. "Your grandmother didn't allow alcohol in her home when she was alive, and we're certainly not going to dishonor her by bringing it in here after she's gone." Susan tucked her tail and carried the six-pack back to her car.

Aunt Lolly sat on the couch, smiling, and seemingly happy to be in the midst of the flurry of family and friends.

"Oh, this is such a nice party," she said. "What are we celebrating?"

"Well, Aunt Lolly," my mother gently reminded her. "We've just come from your sister, Frieda's, funeral. She passed away a few days ago."

"Oh, no!" she exclaimed. "Why didn't somebody tell me? Oh, I can't believe Sistah is gone! I'm gonna miss her so much. We used to have the best time. She'd sit there (pointing to Grandmommie's worn recliner), and I'd sit here, and we'd just laugh and have the best time. Oh, I'm just so upset that nobody told me she died. Why didn't somebody tell me?"

For a few moments, Aunt Lolly sobbed quietly, and mumbled to herself, "I just don't understand why nobody told me Sistah died." Then, she opened her purse to retrieve what we were sure would be a tissue but, instead, was a blue washcloth upon which she wiped her tears and blew her nose. My sisters and I chuckled discreetly and wondered what other oddities she might be carrying around.

Shortly, Aunt Lolly forgot her grief, and began smiling again and telling everyone how nice it was to see them (whoever they were!).

"Oh, just look at all this good food. Aren't we so blessed?" she asked.

"Yes, we sure are," my Aunt Darla assured her.

"Now, what's the occasion?" she asked. "Is it somebody's birthday?"

"No, Aunt Lolly, remember, your sister, Frieda, passed away. We've all been to the funeral, and the family is here now sharing a meal."

"What? You mean Sistah passed away and nobody told me? Oh, I can't believe she's gone. Why did you all keep it from me? Oh, I'm gonna miss her so much. She used to sit over there (again, pointing to the recliner), and I'd sit over here, and we'd just laugh and have the best time."

"I know, Aunt Lolly," Aunt Darla consoled, as she hugged her and kissed her forehead. "We're all going to miss Mama. Aunt Lolly dried her tears with the blue washcloth.

This scenario played out for several hours, and as grief-stricken as we all were, it became so hilarious that some of us had to leave the room to hide our belly laughs. We ultimately decided to spare Aunt Lolly the truth and told her that it was a birthday party. Her smile returned, and the washcloth went back in her purse.

A week later, Uncle Jack and I went to the cemetery to haul away the dead flower arrangements, and to make sure the headstone had been properly placed. "Aunt Lolly's house is just down the road. Let's stop by and say hello to her while we're here," Uncle Jack suggested. "Alright," I agreed.

We knocked at her door, scoffing at the notion of her still living alone in her current state of advanced dementia.

"Well, Jack, hello! Come right on in," she greeted, hugging and kissing each of us.

"This is Gwen," Uncle Jack told her. "Your niece Janelle's oldest daughter."

"Why, sure," she said hesitantly. "I know Gwen."

"Good to see you, Aunt Lolly," I said.

"What in the world are y'all doing out this way?" she asked.

"We've been down to the cemetery and just thought we'd stop by and see you while we were here," Uncle Jack told her.

"The cemetery?" she asked. "Who died?"

"Oh, good Lord," Uncle Jack mumbled to me, rolling his eyes. "Here we go again."

Aunt Lolly died seven months after Grandmommie Frieda (her beloved "Sistah") had passed away. It's been twenty years now, but my family's recollection of this story still evokes laughter, and I think of Aunt Lolly every time I see a blue washcloth or a strawberry cake.

Not For Whites Only

"You niggers better get outta here," two men screamed from the highway above our campsite at Lake Lanier, Georgia. It was a Friday night, in early fall 1967, when I and other adults from Mennonite House in Atlanta arrived to enjoy an outing at the public campground with ten African-American boys. While we had been setting up camp and starting a cook fire the men had parked beside the road and verbally accosted us. We were startled. The boys had been camping with us at Lake Allatoona and other campgrounds in Georgia, and we had even been to a Mennonite Church Camp near Meridian, Mississippi. This was the first time we had experienced such extreme hostility. Misgivings about the safety of the boys mixed with our anger. We had not intended this outing to confront racism.

We puzzled as to what to do, but when the cars drove away, we shrugged and continued to prepare dinner. Mary, famous both for her cooking and organizational skills, was in

charge. Mary, her husband Tim, and I were a part of a
Mennonite "unit" of eight young people in our twenties who
had come to Atlanta from the north for voluntary service in
an African-American neighborhood. Since the Mennonite
religion is pacifistic, this assignment counted as my
compulsory military service when many males were still in
Viet Nam.

Our main house, in the middle of Old Fourth Ward,
was near Ebenezer Baptist Church where Martin Luther King,
Jr. preached. But three of us men lived nearby in a duplex on
Irwin Street, a section characterized by low income, crowding
and the street teeming with children and adolescents. The
upstairs, other than our bedroom and small kitchen, was also
always packed with kids and teenagers. The other half of the
duplex served as a small recreation center with ping pong
tables and other games; behind the duplex we worked with
some of the larger boys to clean up a junk filled lot and to
install a basketball goal. We also had three African-American
students from Morehouse College living with us, and Bob,
one of them, was along on the trip as another adult presence.
So it was from this setting that we had organized some
adolescents, ten to twelve years of age, for this camping trip.

For the trip we had loaded up the Ford van, belonging
to Mennonite House, and an old Rambler belonging to Mary
and Tim. We had set out for a place we hadn't visited before,
on the west side of Buford Dam in Forsyth County. The kids
had been amazed as we drove over the dam. "Man, that's a
long ways down," one said in awe as they looked down over
the deep concrete side, on our way to the park and
campground. When we reached the west side of the dam we
circled down the drive to the campground and picked a site.
It was here that an hour later our peaceful campground was
invaded by the hateful screams from the road above us. We

were still discussing what had happened when some of the kids, who had been canoeing out on the lake, raced back to the camp frightened and out of breath. We soon pieced together their story. A motor boat had repeatedly sped toward them, and then swerved at the last minute. Just then, the cars that had driven off returned again to hurl their abusive insults down the hill. When the cars drove away this time, we adults consulted and agreed that if they returned a third time, I would talk to the men to determine if the threat was as serious as it was beginning to appear.

I took a short cut up the steep embankment to the road and hid behind some scrubby trees to wait. When they drove up again, I stepped out, walked up to the car, petrified, but determined, and asked what the problem was. They were startled by my sudden appearance and immediately lost a bit of their bluster.

"Well, we just wanted to warn you that we don't allow niggers here in Forsyth County. We make sure that none of them spend the night here. People say that the last one, who tried to spend the night here, left our county feet first." They said there were other people who would try to make trouble for us if we tried to spend the night. While the ones I was speaking to wouldn't do anything to hurt us, they said, they only wanted to warn us that it was not safe because of what these other people might do. I thanked them for letting us know. As subtly as possible I wrote their license numbers down in my note book.

Then I returned to the camp where the frightened group waited anxiously for me. I reported what had been said and that it was clear it was time to leave. It would have been irresponsible to subject these youth to such danger. We loaded up the van and car and started back across the dam. The men who had yelled at us followed. The Rambler began to sputter as we approached the other side and when we reached the far side of the dam, we pulled off to examine the motor. The car needed more help than we could give. It was getting dark. The local cars that had followed us had passed, turned around and drove past us again.

We found a roadside spot, just off the road, where we could push the car, and all thirteen of us packed into the van for the return trip to Atlanta. As the van started to move, everyone was tense and silent.

My mind went back four years earlier to Neshoba County, Mississippi, when three civil rights workers were stopped on the highway and murdered, after visiting a burned African-American church. My brother had been involved with Mickey Schwerner, one of the three, in rebuilding other burned African-American churches. Now, after some anxious minutes, the trailing cars turned around and my terror began to ease as it seemed that we had avoided a similar fate.

As the trailing cars turned around and the tension subsided, the boys began talking. "Do you think they really would have killed us if we had stayed?" The adults wondered the same question. All of us had been frightened, and after rehashing what had happened for a while we turned to music to ease our fears. As we got to I-85 heading toward the safety of Irwin Street, we sang lustily one of the boys' favorites about the great Chicago fire of 1871:

> Late last night while we were all in bed,
> Old Lady O'Leary set her lantern in her shed,
> And when the cow kicked it over she bowed her head
> and said,
> It's gonna be a hot time in the old town tonight.

Then it was "We Are Climbing Jacob's Ladder," another favorite. Our spirits and courage revived by the singing, we arrived back at Irwin Street. This was a block with drugs, violence and crime but after Forsyth County we all felt we were finally safe at home.

The next day, a Saturday, some of us began calling friends with whom we had been involved in civil rights. Al Henry, a white minister who had lost his pastor's job in Birmingham because of his stands on integration, was a good friend and a civil rights activist. He introduced us to John McGowan, an African-American organizer in the civil rights movement. I was among a small group which met and discussed what we should do. After leaving the campground that night so as not to jeopardize the boys, we had no intention of letting the situation go unchallenged. Meanwhile, two members of our unit, Tim and Waldie, went back to rescue the car. The car was gone! Fearing the worst, they reported it stolen and watched as the sheriff wrote down a different description than they had given. When they challenged him he said gruffly "Are you trying to make trouble?" Later the state police recovered the car, but it never worked well again.

We decided to return in force in two weeks seeking the attention of the media as our protection. The underground newspaper, the *Great Speckled Bird*, reported what had happened and soon I was interviewed by the *Atlanta Constitution* as well. Word spread in the civil rights community and among our friends. A meeting at Quaker House, organized for a different forum, soon segued into a discussion of our plans.

Beforehand, we returned to talk to public officials in Forsyth County. We walked into the sheriff's office, which looked like a set out of the movie, *In the Heat of the Night*. The cigar chewing sheriff looked at the five of us and said gruffly that he could only talk to me since I was the one who had asked for the meeting. The others would have to wait outside the office with the door closed. Well, okay—I guess, I agreed nervously. I had just begun to tell the sheriff and his two deputies what had happened, when the folks waiting outside got concerned. The door edged open and Charlie Webster, always dressed nattily in a suit and tie, pushed his way in. He was followed by the other three. We finished telling the sheriff and his deputies what had happened at the campground and told them of our plans. We would be returning, and we wanted to be assured that they would protect us while we exercised our right to enjoy the park as an integrated group.

"Well, I can't be sure that we will be able to protect you. Folks feel pretty strong about these things here in Forsyth County," he said. The two deputies shifted in their chairs. One took out a large knife from his pocket, unclasped it and began to clean his finger nails.

"You need to uphold the law, isn't that your role?" I insisted.

"Well we'll do what we can but we can't assure you that you will be safe." We waited. He shrugged. The two deputies looked away. Hardly reassured, we shook hands and left.

The Forsyth Chamber of Commerce and the Forsyth newspaper began calling Mennonite House, upset about the unfavorable light being cast on their community. The newspaper editor called me to ask if I could identify the people who had threatened us. I gave him the license numbers I had written down. He called me the next day to say, "We have identified the owners and they don't have a net worth of $1,000 between them. They are poor ignorant people and their conduct should not reflect on the good people of Forsyth County."

"But the good people, as you call them, have allowed this climate to exist. The leaders need to lead and change what is considered acceptable behavior," I countered.

The Saturday afternoon for our revisit arrived and a group began to gather in a church parking lot. There were progressive religious people, civil rights activists, students, and professors. We were a diverse group but we did not allow children for what was potentially a dangerous mission. I was driving the van again as we pulled out of the lot with a caravan of cars following, on the road to Forsyth County. When we arrived at the camp, several of us, including a reporter from the *Atlanta Constitution*, set up a game of horseshoes, but the game was interrupted by a shower and we scurried to our cars. By the time the shower passed, we needed to start setting up camp. Another group of cars, including our leader, John McGowan, arrived late because they had had trouble finding the campground. He scolded me for leaving Atlanta before the entire caravan was ready. I was embarrassed and apologized for my carelessness.

Around seventy-five people set up tents or other accommodations. After we shared a meal, we gathered to organize for the night. An Episcopal priest who had been a Marine took charge of security. "We need to keep lookouts posted around the perimeter," he said. "If there is any encroachment during the night, the camp has to be alerted."

"And what the hell do we do when we are alerted?" I wondered to myself.

John seemed to read my mind and pulled me off to the side. "I don't want people to know this, but I did bring some protection. We are not going to be sitting ducks if someone attacks us with guns."

A little later a car with Morehouse students, including Bob, pulled in to join us, and as I spoke with them I pretended not to notice the gun on the seat. I was a practitioner of non-violence like Dr. King and Mahatma Gandhi. On the other hand ... well, I confess that I did feel a tad more secure knowing what I knew.

Someone had brought a portable TV and we watched the evening news. "A group of people from Atlanta are putting their lives on the line in Forsyth County tonight," the reporter began. Sitting around as a group in the dimly lit clearing, surrounded by trees, darkness and the sounds of the night, I shivered as I felt true fear. However, no one doubted we had to take this action.

But the night passed without incident. We awoke in the early morning to share breakfast. We told stories of the long night, sleepless for many. Soon it was time for the trek back to Atlanta for what remained of the weekend.

On Monday I returned to teach my seventh-grade social studies classes. The students, mostly African-Americans, were buzzing about their teacher being on television. Oh, and what he had been doing was pretty cool too.

SARAH KEGLEY

Thin Soup

Suddenly, my thin life was thick. It had filled up seemingly overnight. I had landed in Madrid eight months earlier, with five suitcases, two cats, and no "baggage." I had been able to flit about the city, with the ease of invisibility and a rhythm all my own. I ducked into museums when I noticed I was standing in front of them; I ducked into bars when I needed a swig. I sat on park benches and sidewalk benches and bus-stop benches and watched the people, never feeling the need to pretend I was waiting on someone, or about to read something, or searching for my bus pass. I had no need to feel important. I just sat there; I just "was."

I shopped at my leisure, often buying nothing but a ripe piece of fruit. I stayed out 'til 2 a.m., because I could; it was normal, even for a woman alone. I took the train places no one knew about. I read whole books.

The conversion to this fantasy existence had been timely. Before I left for Madrid, the last night I was in

Atlanta, my friends were gathered on my front porch, a summer night with mosquitoes and fireflies, all of us on the floor, seated in low-to-the-ground folding chairs they'd brought over. The U-Haul was sitting in the driveway.

That night, one friend asked me, and the others fell silent as they listened for my reply, "What scares you the most about this move?" I looked to the air, and thought for a moment: "Oh, the job I guess."

I wasn't expecting their laughter, but laugh they did. When they saw the bewilderment on my face, one said, "Good heavens, I'd be scared to death about meeting people and making friends," and everyone nodded, saying "yeah ... me too ... ."

I still remember feeling that string pulling on the back of my head, that feeling when you are about to roll your eyes, and stopped myself. Then another friend piped up, "No, one thing about Sarah is that she never has a hard time making friends, so that wouldn't scare her." That was nice to hear about myself, but I had honestly never considered it.

But there was also a feeling that I couldn't state aloud—one of utter relief. Yes, I was happy to be leaving these friends behind. I couldn't wait to get an ocean between me and them and their drama queen details, their overbooked lives, and their constant need for my special brand of front-porch therapy. Each had, in their own way, been standing on my last nerve for months.

A little person inside me was tap dancing to "yippideedoodah."

Those first few months in Madrid are a blur. There was the time change, and the work was pretty constant, and just learning to maneuver my neighborhood streets of *Madrid Antiguo*, Historic Madrid, without walking in circles for hours took up much of my energy. Then there was the grocery store—a chore that I used to adore—which suddenly became an exercise in interpreting cultural behavior, not to mention vocabulary. Unlocking the magic blend of logic and creativity that would help me find the things I needed became my daily meditation:

> *Olivo* is a tree, not an olive. A *pudding* is a piece of cake. The milk is in the cereal aisle, in a cardboard "brick" carton, not refrigerated. And there is no vanilla ice cream. It's labeled vanilla, but it's sweet cream with no flavoring. There's no vanilla extract, and there's no peanut butter; stop searching! Going to the market without makeup will guarantee you stares, and standing patiently in line will get you absolutely nowhere .... .

Little lessons came every day. After ordering *pudding* twice in two months, and slapping my hand to my forehead thinking, "Not again!" I began to count. It took seven times of my ordering *pudding* for me to remember: *It's pound cake. It's not a light, healthy yogurt. It's pound cake.* "One, two-hoo, three," I heard the little owl in the Tootsie Pop commercial.

The re-discovery of books did much to charm these months of invisibility. An expat living in Japan wrote that, because he was unable to understand all the jumbled sounds of Japanese that filled the metro, he was able to concentrate on whole books in a way he had not experienced since he was a child. I, too, would lose myself completely to the stories, blithely unaffected by my environment, no matter how close the next pair of shoulders, how many elbows I took in the back, or how loud the screeching of the train was on the tracks. I discovered Barbara Kingsolver, first through the *Bean Trees*, then *Animal Dreams*. I read Adriana Trigiani's trilogy, and laughed out loud in response to her take on the people of the Appalachian Mountains, mountains that I knew so well. Even at home, I would lie on the couch and read, while the European buzz of scooters on the street below came and went, and the trickle and swoosh of the fountain in the plaza danced in the background. These sounds meant nothing to me then, except peace.

My lack of a social life of obligation allowed me to spend time in the Institute Library—precious *time*, that thing that no one *has*—looking at books, touching them, reading paragraphs, perusing covers. Grace Paley became my new fixation; I would take her home on the bus at night, cradling the hardback cover of her books as if a bead of her soul had somehow been cast off and wound up conserved within those pages. Who was she? *I had time to wonder.* Why hadn't I heard of her before? And what about me? Why was I discovering books, *of all things*, books, in this fancy new city of mine? Books in English, no less.

Being on the metro was something to look forward to. I didn't even care about the instant brand of "foreigner" I would receive when people saw me reading in English; I just read.

Yes, there were times when people would break through the sound barrier of "Spanish and city" that surrounded me, and directly address me with a question, or ask me what I was reading, or ask if I were American. Then, as politely as possible, I would nod, and pretend not to understand them and dive back into my new world of stories. "Set in my ways" in the first six months of metro riding! I could hear my grandmother laughing ... *"Don't get too set in your ways,"* she always reminded us. *"Ever. About anything."* Oh, well.

On more than one of those occasions I met a friend. Once, on the metro reading, and feeling very set in my ways, a voice behind me said, "You're giving yourself away." *Damn ... English.* I'm instantly distracted. The first thought in my head was fickle: *Who are you? Go away. You will get no part of me today.*

Then he said it again and, without meaning to, I jerked around to see his face. A tall, muscular black man cloaked in a grey overcoat faced me, smiling down at me. A very pleasant and friendly face. Suddenly, I wasn't in my fantasy city anymore, barreling through the streets on a fast train, lost in someone else's story. His voice had taken me somewhere else, somewhere inviting, somewhere familiar.

Home.

I hesitated, not speaking, and he continued, "You're giving yourself away, reading that book in English. Everyone's going to know you're American."

"I could be British" was my instant retort, proving that I wasn't.

"Or you could be Australian, or Irish," he retorted right back.

We laughed at each other, bringing my guard down, and we chatted for the rest of the ride. It wasn't the last time I saw him. He was new to the city, an Embassy employee. A former Marine, acting now as something of a bodyguard, but without all the 24/7 demands that bodyguards usually have. He had the build for it: somewhere around 6'5", maybe 220 pounds, and just plain big, he would have scared me if we'd been meeting in a dark alley, or, as it were, in the underbellies of the Embassy's secret tunnels guarding some seemingly regular Joe. I'd run.

But talking to him that night, he was a gentle giant, with a voice I had to incline my head to hear at times, and a friendly, angelic face, unlikely as it sounds for a bodyguard and right there on the metro, jerking and tumbling its way through the corridors of the city's underground.

So, no, I wasn't alone a lot of the time, but I was *by myself* during those first months, working out all these new tasks of daily existence, absorbing Spanish as fast as I could, and reading in English like there was no tomorrow. And it didn't occur to me until someone asked me, around December sometime, "Do you miss your friends in Atlanta?" And I blurted out "No!" before I could stop myself. I had to backtrack a bit, because it sounded so bad, and this guy was becoming a friend, after all.

But I realized that it was true—I didn't miss them. I did enjoy anonymity. I was soaking up the city and just letting it cook into me, a stew of me.

It's easy—and delightful—to save it all for yourself sometimes. To spend months and months soaking up everything and giving away nothing. It's ironic to me that I would call this part my "thin" life.

And one day, and I don't remember when, exactly, but suddenly one day, it had filled up again. Someone called to invite me to a movie. Shortly after, someone else invited me to dinner. Then I met a man, and he started to fill up my precious life spaces. And then his family, calling me for Sunday lunch, that age-old Spanish tradition, week after week. That wonderful empty Sunday afternoon I had learned to devour was suddenly bulldozed into a three-hour lunch full of chatter and questions and yelling and grotesque amounts of food. And just as suddenly, my colleagues began to call on me for every little thing.

Don't misunderstand me—I'm not complaining. These are wonderful people, these characters who jumped into my simmer. These are my friends now. This is what my life turned into; it is what happens, if you're lucky.

But the freedom of being "thin soup" for a while, flitting in and out of bars and cafés, having ice cream for breakfast, standing in front of the Museum talking to Velazquez, staring up at the marble Cervantes, talking to the grumpy old men in the park who feed the pigeons and the women who yell at them ...

Baby, that's heaven.

Sweet Tea

My husband Danny and I planned a home birth for our child who was due on the Summer Solstice, 1994. Cory came, however, in his own sweet time, by C-section, a few hours past Independence Day. Waiting those two extra weeks, we laughed that this kid had a sense of humor, and noted the most useful maxim I know: expect the unexpected. It came home to me eighteen summers later.

The season suits Cory. Like summer, he is pleasantly languid, and a big fan of unscheduled time and overly sweet southern tea. Our trio has long celebrated each summer's start with the year's first pitcher of that favorite brew, good old Lipton, laced with ample simple syrup— enough to give the local hero soft drink, Coca-Cola, a good run for its super sweet money. I savor the ritual as much as the tea.

We drink it on our back deck, one that for years overlooked rampant weeds, until we installed a pond and self-circulating stream, and a gravel path amid boulders and blue hydrangeas. I stare at it often; its order and illusion of control calm me.

But on Summer Solstice of 2012, I forgot to make tea, and I had no time for garden gazing. I had driven Cory to a mall fourteen miles from home. When I returned, exhausted from that excursion, brewing tea slipped my mind. In hindsight, this slip in ritual was a harbinger of change which I would struggle to embrace.

On that first day of summer, Cory committed what some called juvenile lunacy: he bought a motorcycle. As a teenager, I had loved riding with cousins on the backs of their bikes, so, since Cory had taken a motorcycle safety class, was cautious to the nth degree, and was two weeks shy of eighteen, Danny and I shrugged and took his decision as our first split with him on where to spend money; it was, after all, his cash.

Who knew, when Cory was an industrious six-year-old, squeezing a hundred lemons by hand with his dad (and in later years, with a friend), that his lemonade stand during annual neighborhood festivals would start a savings account that, along with gifts, earnings from dog-sitting, carpentry, and tree-climbing support gigs, would eventually yield a sum that he could trade for this iconic toy.

Slowly I trailed Cory from the mall where he'd exchanged his savings for speed and adventure, wishing I could protect him. I was also trying to take a picture of this moment with my cellphone, so, in his first few minutes on that thing, I practically hit him myself. Cory had stopped at the parking lot's stop sign, and I didn't notice I was still rolling until I was inches from his tailpipe. I slammed on my brakes hard enough to scatter my purse contents on the floor. Cory didn't flinch. Seeing him so close, so vulnerable—and apparently oblivious to my near-miss—was sobering.

What a weird fourteen miles that was following him home: watching him, losing sight of him, seeing him again, and then finally losing him altogether on a winding back road. It ceased feeling fun. After I'd not seen him for a long while, my smart phone tracking app indicated Cory was *on the freeway*, contrary to our explicit agreement. That wasn't like Cory. "Oh ... my ... God," I thought, "the only way he'd be on the interstate is if he were in an ambulance."

At the time, it didn't seem far-fetched, being he was a new rider. So I got on the interstate looking for him, and, for ambulances. Mostly I sat in five o'clock traffic, pounding the steering wheel and leaving phone messages for Danny and Cory. Finally, Cory called. He had ridden via surface streets, as we'd agreed, and he was home. I arrived almost an hour after I'd lost sight of him, spent.

When I posted on Facebook a photo of Cory with his new Honda, I anticipated a few of the usual thumbs up "likes;" instead an onslaught of comments ensued, mostly cautions on the hazards of riding a motorcycle. I no longer knew where I stood, and I felt terrified of how fast this thing was capable of going—life, that is—and how little I would now know about Cory's.

At the same time, I felt faintly envious. Cory had something thrilling, and emblematic of independence. Those same sentiments had marked my many seasons of nurturing him since infancy, doing something different with my mothering role than most of my friends, witnessing his growth up close all day, into adulthood. I had done my best at what had felt most natural. But what to do now?

That summer would be the last of our family's eighteen years as a continuous, tight trio. After August, Cory would be a returning member, coming home from college on vacations. Already I was looking back, wistfully, as if I hadn't been with him enough.

Yet I had spent more hours caring for him than most mothers of my time. Nurturing and teaching him at home his whole life had been my mainstay. And though I sometimes felt isolated, it was the most stimulating work of my varied occupations, from pediatric nursing to political campaign-managing to directing the Downtown Branch of the Atlanta History Center to part-time college teaching. For job satisfaction, at-home mothering and tutoring trumped them all—and paid its dividends in giggles.

So, Cory's acceptance in 2012 into the rigorous engineering program at Georgia Tech was an endorsement, of sorts, of our years of work. It was also my pink slip. My role as his original and literal alma mater had ended. I was sad; and, I was thrilled. Cory was nearly launched. I hadn't, however, expected how close to literal his launch would be, nor how trying.

When Cory had first mentioned wanting a motorcycle, I'd been surprised, given his cautious, quiet nature. His bicycle and rapid transit had always been adequate. "Think about it Mom," explained my used-to-be-toddler, who always had tools, real and pretend; who made imaginary mechanical devices, such as "an automatic handkerchief press" that he "operated" weekly when he was three as I folded the rest of the laundry. "It's a *machine.*" Cory paused and then grinned as I took this in, "And," he finished with a flourish, arms apart, "it's practical: it gets seventy miles to the gallon."

"I see," I'd said, and I did. But not for long. One neighbor, an insurance executive to whom I told Cory's choice, stopped loading his car, and fixed his eyes on mine before speaking. "You know," he said, in a low tone, "statistics show 100% risk for motorcycle accidents. It's only a matter of time." He shut the trunk, got in his car, and then finished in a higher, happy octave, "Of course, they may not *all* be *bad* accidents." He smiled and waved as he drove off.

Lest we were unenlightened, friends shared with us their "bad accident" tales. I was neither for nor against motorcycles; I was a mother grappling with what it meant to trust. When Cory would tell me how fun it felt to lean in and corner, I loved seeing his wide smile and dimples. How could I not share his exuberance? When I was his age, I'd learned to drive my dad's Triumph Spitfire. Driving cars with stick shifts and V-6 engines still exhilarates me— the better to rev the RPMs. The first few times Cory would ride away, I'd watch from the driveway, waving and feeling that thrill long after I could see him.

But sometimes, when I'd happen to see him prepare, strapping on that heavy helmet, pulling on thick gloves, and, even in the summer heat, zipping his padded jacket designed to protect him from road rash, or from breaking ribs if he "spilled," it was too much like combat readiness. Tears would fill my eyes and I would go inside to busy myself. Once I thought of that children's story *Are You My Mother?* about a baby bird tumbling out of the nest, and I wished I were a bird. Bird brains don't wonder if their fledglings are about to die.

Danny and I had prepared Cory for adulthood, but apparently I hadn't prepared myself. We had educated Cory in all we thought important, from manners and classical studies to handling shop machines and making meals. We had deemed Cory graduated; yet, I felt prematurely sidelined—and now, less comfortable with letting him pick his risks.

I admit, she is a beautiful blue, white, and red riding machine, and well proportioned, too, that Honda I nicknamed Rhonda—though calling her by name seems inappropriate when asking Cory if he's ridden her lately. Rhonda is a sport-bike, also known as a "crotch rocket," capable of launch and thrust that I haven't cared to learn about. Cory contends that her smallish 250 cc engine eliminates her from crotch-rocket status. Nonetheless, my imagination gyrates.

Somewhere during those fourteen miles home, I recalled another of Cory's rides, on the other kind of bike. It had been an unseasonably warm February day, and we had been outdoors most of the afternoon, Cory comfortable in jeans and no jacket; just a navy cotton turtleneck. He was four years old, and trying to ride a two wheeler, his white helmet bright in the sunlight. For the umpteenth time, I was running alongside, holding on to him as he wobbled. This time, though, he pedaled faster, and more furiously, like he'd done it forever. So, I let go. I let go, and he rode on, laughing; his slender back grew narrower as he blended into the distance, all by himself. I had to call to him, grinning, to come back before he got too far.

The first autumn of Cory's life, when he was two months old, I had not been able to let go, to leave him even part-time at the daycare of Georgia State University where I had loved my teaching job. I couldn't drop him off with strangers just so I could teach someone else, perhaps missing his first words, or, his first hard fall. Compared with the chance to be home nurturing a brand new being, teaching Logic and Critical Thinking now sounded arid. I wanted to spend mornings playing peek-a-boo in bed. I was the only one with the title "Cory's Mom," and I wanted to embrace it all day.

In Spanish, the question to ask instead of, "What do you do for a living?" is, "¿A qué se dedica?"—"To what do you dedicate yourself?" I had dedicated myself to my family: mothering became my way to be. I hadn't known how joyful, nor how painful, such dedication could become, until I had twice watched him ride away.

The last thing I'd considered during those demanding eighteen years was that I was working hard to eliminate my own job. When Cory first left for college, I had to avoid his bedroom doorway; his vacated room left me empty. I felt unexpectedly bereft. It's like we all know we'll die but we're still taken aback when anyone does.

My job that autumn became remote mom, on-call. My duties were to counsel Cory when he asked, hug him hard through all that safety gear, and then let go. Embrace, release, I am getting the hang of it.

On his visits from Georgia Tech, I ask him to always check his rearview mirror; you never know what to expect if your own mother once almost rear-ended you. The rest of his adventure, I leave to him.

Now when Cory pulls away, engine revving, I watch him leave, but not for long. Before Rhonda's roar has faded, I retreat to the back deck to write. As I sit under the huge overhanging branches, my mind sometimes meanders to an image of Cory on his motorcycle. I smile as I see him lean into the curve, his ample back broadening that red padded jacket; and, on the back of his helmet, in reflective gold tape, glint two large interlocking letters: "GT," the insignia of his next alma mater.

I'm content with emeritus status; I have time now to work at my own pace, sipping tea. It's sweet, but not too sweet.

Robin

"Jim? You need to read the letter in the kitchen," my wife said, as I pushed through the door with my briefcase. She skipped my usual arrival-home hug and led me to the counter. I puzzled over the Portland postmark, then pulled some cheap stationary from the card-sized envelope she had already opened. The unfamiliar child-like scrawl was difficult to follow.

"You've read this? What is it?"

Tracy nodded toward the pages: "Just ... keep your mind open."

I dropped onto the adjacent stool, and read on: "Dear Jimmy, you must be surprised to get this letter after all this time, but there are some things I have to tell you. I have thought of you a lot over the years ..." Too curious, I flipped to the last page—signed "Robin."

"Who is she!—You know I've had no affairs ... Does she claim she's my love-child?"

"Go on."

I loosened my tie and read on: "I have enjoyed reading your cards and notes over the years, and they make me feel you will understand. Here is the news: I have come to realize that I am not the Robert you have known. I am a woman, Robin Ste. Regis."

Robert? From high school? Robert had probably been not only the smartest kid, but the oddest at our Catholic school. He was born big-footed, heavy-jawed and with a hawkish nose, yet he apparently chose to wear horn-rimmed glasses and the most distinctive hair at the school. Although this was the era of the hippie, St. Leo required boys to wear a blazer and tie and to keep their hair clear of their ears and shoulders. These restraints were no impediment to Robert— he just let his kinky hair rise, Marge Simpson-like, adding several inches to his already tall frame. The teachers in math and science couldn't keep up with him, so the school sent him to the university to get those classes. We shared English and social studies, where he stood out for his mild but insightful comments.

I got to know Robert better when he joined our chess team. With his massive head and academic reputation, we expected him to prove a genius at the board, yet he turned out to be only a passable player. The capabilities and limitations of the pieces and the near-infinite tree of possible positions fascinated him, but he lacked competitive drive. He adopted an eccentric opening known as Santasiere's Folly, in which the player walks his king into the center of the fray, and would consider the gambit a success if it produced a single win in twenty tries.

Robert was friendly when approached, but was slow to offer up much about his interests and enthusiasms. Aside from his intellect and appearance, he seemed like most of the kids, devout and dutiful, and attached to a large, tight-knit family. Unpretentious, he was liked by both students and teachers. He was one of the few boys on the staff of the school's literary journal, and he was eventually made its editor. I had written a review of the Firesign Theater's off-the-wall comedy LP, "How Can You Be in Two Places at Once When You Are Not Anywhere at All" as an assignment, and he surprised me by publishing it. He found my commentary on the record's utter nonsense slyly subversive, and it drew us together. I, awkward and uncool, was glad to have Robert to chat with between classes. I remember being taken aback when he spoke to me of his love of musicals, *Oklahoma!, Guys and Dolls,* and all that. When *Grease* came out on Broadway, he travelled to see the show repeatedly—he could barely contain himself from singing "Look at me, I'm Sandra Dee" in class. All this in the age of psychedelic rock, when most kids showed nothing but contempt for that sort of staged sentimentality.

Eventually, Robert graduated and headed to a top university, to study physics, then to another to get his Ph.D. I had last seen him thirty years ago, at his wedding to Cindy. After that, it was mostly a Christmas-newsletter relationship, and Tracy and I kept track as he took a university position, raised two sons, and much later adopted twins.

This letter made it clear that Robert believed he was born into the wrong body. Or, I guess I should say "Robin," as he implored at its end. After digesting this revelation for a few days, I wrote him, that is, her (it was tough to get my mind around this) a note back. Mercifully, in my note I could use the pronoun "you." I wrote something to the effect that I was glad he/she had been in touch and had learned this about him(her)self, and I hoped that (s)he would benefit from the discovery. Frankly, I was not sure why I had gotten the letter.

Then, Tracy and I both received invitations to become Facebook friends. There we read my old classmate's frequent posts, mostly on politics, recipes and knitting. Later came an email: "I will be attending a convention in Atlanta in a few weeks and would love to see you." Tracy, without consultation, fired one back immediately, offering our home for the stay. Oh, well, that's just like her. And how bad could the brief visit be?

At the airport, Tracy and I waited at the top of a long escalator and tried to spot our guest among the hundreds of passengers moving toward the baggage claim. The flight from Portland was listed as "on ground," but we stood there for a very long time. As each person filed by, I wondered if I would be able to pick out my old school chum. I scanned the faces of each of the older men, wondering if he could be the one.

Then I realized that, because of gender reassignment, I had better check out folks regardless of their dress. This guy could be him, or is he too old? Would Robert be that wrinkled? Bald? Wearing a wig? Could that tall well-dressed woman be the one?—My friend would never look like that, right? No one, regardless of sex, resembled the Robert I remembered. But surely we all had changed in 30 years, and he … she … more than most!

After forty minutes of this ridiculousness, we saw the familiar face approaching us, virtually unchanged. The hair was a dead giveaway too, graying now, but in the old unkempt bush. The Robert I recalled had been an untidy dresser, and this was altered only slightly now: flat clunky sandals such as I owned, unstylish jeans, a cotton tee with a slightly unmasculine scoop, and a tiny gold chain. We exchanged hugs, Tracy enthusiastically, and then me, for lack of knowing what else to do.

In the car on the way home, our guest showed no reluctance to discuss the transformation from "Robert" to "Robin." Not long after the start of college, a secret alter ego emerged that yearned to be called Robin Ste. Regis. "I got a credit card in that name, imagined using it to buy feminine things, but never really did." On leaving school, Robert's conventional life resumed. There was the marriage to Cindy, the job and their children. When their sons were grown, the empty-nesters decided to foster and then adopt Cambodian twins, now seven years old. Robert's career involved a very obscure corner of the physics world, and when his position was eliminated, opportunities were few. Then, after a year of unemployment, a position opened up in Moscow. Cindy could hardly imagine moving their family to Russia, but agreed that if Robert would go ahead, become acclimated, and make arrangements, they would follow.

Robert told us of several months living there alone in a tiny apartment. "The language, the food, the isolation all disoriented me. One night I had to get out, and went to a party that reeked of pot. I didn't smoke any, but my mind became confused. Leaving, I couldn't control my thoughts. I wandered the streets the rest of the night and much of the next day. Notions overcame me: for most of the time I was convinced I was Jesus Christ, despondent that no one would recognize and listen to me." At last he was stopped and hospitalized. Cindy flew over and took him back to Oregon for treatment. There, a therapist quickly discerned his feminine alter ego and began working with him to understand it. Robert concluded that the only path to restored sanity was to embrace and become Robin Ste. Regis.

We continued our conversations when we arrived home from the airport. Cindy had been, and continued to be, devastated and angry. Their children were confused, and their extended family and most friends were aghast. "They think my gender reassignment is a symptom, not a cure." Divorced and unemployed, Robert scraped together funds to pay for a name change and for difficult proceedings to obtain joint custody of the twins. He succeeded, though, and found an apartment where he kept the kids after school and on alternate weekends. He told us all this as you would bring any old friend current on your doings, and I tried to avoid gasps and grimaces and take it in the same manner.

Everything was not so grim—the little twins were accepting. "They are sweet as can be—tentative at first, but we started cooking and doing crafts, and they liked it." Robert really seemed to be working at this "woman" thing.

Some mutual friends had received letters similar to mine, and confided in me that they thought Robert's actions harmful and rash. And didn't his decisions leave family, friends, and even society, reeling?

What would these people think of me if I could accept Robin? What would they think of me if I could not? Why would Robert so overthrow his life when so much of it had already been lived with conventional success? I thought about the only other case of transgendering that had affected me, my rock idol Pete Townsend's revelation at a similar age that he considered himself a woman. I had thought his announcement pointless. But then the pain and intensity of The Who's music, which had so resonated in my younger and uncertain self, again swept over me: "See Me, Feel Me, Touch Me, Heal Me," a song I had found so elemental that I had searched out every version recorded and assembled them on a cassette stored in my car's player. More of a cry than a song, it had inspired me to break barriers of shyness and express myself. Maybe Townsend and Robert were not so different than me and had only faced steeper challenges.

Now, I had assumed that the convention the next day would be an esoteric physics seminar, but it turned out to be "Southern Comfort," the annual two-day convocation of the region's transgendered and cross-dressed community. It would be my friend's first exposure to such a gathering. Featured, my buddy explained, were seminars ranging from medical procedures, to family negotiations, to personal appearance, even bathroom etiquette. "And I brought my boots for the culminating event: a 10 p.m.-to-closing tour of Atlanta hot spots!"

The only free time would be dinner the following day, and we agreed that we would eat out together. In the car the next evening, Tracy and I were discussing where we should go, when I remembered that the convention hotel contained La Grotta, Atlanta's best Italian dining. On arrival, we parked and went into the hotel's spacious lobby. The scene was an eye-popper! I saw more tall, high-heeled, provocatively dressed and made-up feminine characters than I had ever imagined, and my imagination tends to such things. That they largely were big-boned, wide-shouldered and strong-jawed was only slightly jarring. I did do my best not to stare, and feigned to examine the brochures left on a sofa, touting similar events held around the country.

We finally found our *persona grata*, who had slipped out to look for our car, dressed in another tee, corduroy slacks and nondescript flats. We proceeded to the restaurant, past a vibrant bar where karaoke was in full swing. La Grotta, also, was full of large, well-dressed and bejeweled feminine attendees, either speaking huskily in small groups or sitting with more ordinary-looking family members. I tried to tune them out, as we began to reminisce at our table. We spoke of old times and classmates. Tracy and I heard some about the day's sessions, and our guest confided more about the difficulties of undertaking a feminine identity. Most heart-piercing was the description of the unwillingness of friends and relatives to accept the change. "Of all my family, only one sister and my gay son are speaking with me."

Because of the vaunted club-hopping jaunt, Robert had registered to stay at the hotel that night. On the way home, Tracy asked me, "How do you suppose Robin fits in with that crowd at the convention?"

"Oh, well, there must be a range of them, in all stages of the transition, all types and personalities—at least I hope so."

Before his departure the next day, Robert called to thank us for our kindnesses. "I didn't feel up to the all-night club event, so I spent a quiet evening catching up on Facebook and email. I'm on my way to the airport now— I'm going to visit my dad and will try to talk with him. It could be a disaster, but I have to give it a try."

As I hung up the phone, I thought: what a strange episode this visit had been! But, as I considered it in the following days, I found our informal reunion reassuring. Thirty years had passed, incredible transformations had occurred; yet, mostly, we had picked up like we had never left off. And despite the dramatic revelations, I found that nothing essential in my classmate had changed. This was the same person I had known before: odd, honest and stubborn in high school, now quirky, open and resolved. Hormone treatments had been mentioned, but I didn't ask whether surgery was planned. It made little difference.

What became clear to me was that I was being called upon, in the most desperate way I could imagine, to understand. However the gender reassignment went, she would remain my friend.

And I would thereafter refer to her as Robin.

Our Back Pages

Notes from the Writers

"Ah, but I was so much older then,
I'm younger than that now."
My Back Pages, by Bob Dylan

I GREW UP in a rural Mennonite community in lower Delaware, the youngest of nine children. The Mennonite Church, where my father served as bishop, was the center of our community. Its evangelical mission dominated my early life.

I was fortunate that as I and my siblings matured, many of us broadened our vision. I was an adolescent in the turbulent 50s and in college in the early 60s. As a young adult, I came to Atlanta in the mid-60s, where I was involved working for civil and human rights. I found community, where a creative, inclusive spirit was nurtured. Exercising freedom and choosing untried paths meant that my new family and our friends made mistakes in the process of experiencing success on our terms. My path has been a crooked line: I'd choose it again over a straight and narrow path of conformity.

In my new retirement phase, I've decided to write in order to try to make sense of my life.

Don Bender

MY PIECE "CARL" is dedicated to my brother Joel.

- As a child, he taught me how to fry worms with a magnifying glass.
- As an adult, he has taught me to never neglect your creativity.
- And to respect your craft by calling it what it is —your work.

Chelsea Cook

REBEKAH DURHAM holds a master's degree in Theology, and has worked within various ministries in the United States, Ireland and Kenya.

Wikipedia describes the Toronto Blessing of which she writes in "A Reluctant Evangelist" is a phenomenon arising out of a neocharismatic evangelical Christian church called Catch the Fire in Toronto, Canada, in 1994. According to this source, the Blessing has become known for ecstatic worship, including laughter, shaking and crying, and a gesture called "crunching," consisting of a vomit-like heaving as a reaction to inviting God to cleanse one's emotions. One critic, Hank Hanegraaff asserts that the Blessing entails people being enslaved into altered states of consciousness where they obscure reality and enshrine absurdity.

Attributed to a Toronto Blessing Revival

I TRY TO LIVE by five maxims:

"Expect the unexpected."

"Take nothing personally."

"Be kind."

"Get yourself outside to get outside yourself."

"This too shall pass" (true enough whether the going is tough or triumphant).

I also try to meditate, walk, and write daily, but I don't succeed at those any better than I adhere to my maxims every day. I am happy that my writing mentor June Akers Seese has had unending faith in my work, ever since I walked into her fiction-writing class in January of 1989. With this publication, I give a special shout-out to "June-bug," and to my dog Daisy, who I think meditates daily, and who is the only canine June ever invited to sit on her deck at lunch.

Lori Feig-Sandoval

I DESCEND FROM generations of consummate Southern storytellers. On the last Sunday in August, my maternal grandmother and her eight siblings would gather under ancient shade trees at the old home place in Newnan, Georgia, for the annual family reunion. Though I was too young to appreciate the worth of these gatherings, I couldn't shake my desire to be within earshot of their tall tales and spinning yarns. The laughter drew me in like a cat to a can of tuna. Not even my cousins' pleas to play hide-and-seek in the cornfield could lure me away. It's in my blood—this need to tell my stories, cement family bonds, know whence I came. Since stories fade with the passage of time, I began writing mine down.

I enrolled in the memoir writing class at Callanwolde Fine Arts Center three years ago in an effort to refine my skills and bring order to what I was writing. After the first session, I asked myself, "Who would want to read about my vanilla life?" I'm not famous. I haven't done anything monumental. There have been no great tragedies over which I've triumphed. But, in time, I've come to understand that good memoir writing exposes common threads in our lives, binding us together and making us relatable no matter what our station in life.

Writing my stories reveals to me the things that have made my life worth living. I hope my journey makes for a worthwhile read.

Gwen Filardi

I dedicate my contribution to the greatest storytellers I've ever known
—My Grandmommie and her eight brothers and sisters.

RALPH FREEDMAN was born in Hamburg, Germany, in 1920. A Jewish refugee, he emigrated to England in 1939, where he first worked on a farm in Derbyshire and later as an interpreter in London. He soon joined his father in the United States, and after his mother and brother escaped from Germany through Russia and Japan, his family settled in Seattle.

Ralph studied at the University of Washington, then entered into Army service. He participated in combat in Tunisia and in the invasion of Italy. Post-war, he served in counterintelligence in Austria, an experience that informed his first published novel, *Divided*, in 1948.

His academic career included a Masters in Philosophy from Brown and a Ph.D. in Comparative Literature from Yale. Ralph later published important and successful biographies of Hermann Hesse and Ranier Maria Rilke.

Returning to fiction, Ralph has published *Rue the Day*, based on his experience in the McCarthy-era, which won the Indie Award for historical fiction in 2010.

Ralph Freedman is Professor Emeritus, Princeton University.

I WAS SIX OR SEVEN when I wrote my first essay. It was a composition about Harriet Tubman. I was in Ms. Vandenburgh's second grade class, and we had to dress up and read our essays in front of the entire school. So there I stood, skinny and plain, wearing my mom's denim skirt, which hung down to my ankles, a white shirt and red scarf tied tightly around my stubby plaits. I, the lone Harriet Tubman, amidst a class full of Betsy Rosses.

My life has never made sense that way. I've always been set apart. Yet, when nothing makes sense writing always does. My pen woos me, finds me and fills me. It is my medicine and my cure. Discovering my truth is never difficult when I yield to its power. And like Harriet, it protects me, rescues me and provides me safe passage from life's carnage. And once safely delivered, it sets me free.

Shani Godwin

FOR ME, WRITING is a way to lose and rework time, a vehicle to plunder the past for meaning. I go back to make sense of feelings and mantras that dog me now. Sometimes I relive a scene with the same helpless sensations, but eventually I step out and assess with a safer look, from a distance. When I stop typing, I see discoveries on a page about myself in context, about my parents in theirs, through words that demystify my hauntings. Finally, I emerge lighter in the belly, having untangled the leaden knots held hostage for years.

Ellen Jones

✻   ✻   ✻

An Atlanta native, Ellen Jones wrote for *Brown's Guide to Georgia* as associate editor, traveling and writing about the State. She later became editor of the Office of Publications at Georgia Institute of Technology. As a freelance writer, she published articles *in Southern Homes, Georgia Journal, Inside Northside, Inside Buckhead, and Alabama* magazines. Currently she is a fitness instructor, sometime artist and re-emerging writer. She lives in Atlanta with her husband, two sons, and a rescue mutt named Georgia.

I LOVE TO LISTEN TO STORIES. Around the kitchen table, on the front porch, on the *back* porch, or by the fireplace. I come from a long line of story-tellers, mountain people who know the gift of a good yarn.

First international travel, with Dad, 1971

My love of language and adventure was sealed through the nightly story-telling by my father, who never needed a book to put us to bed. My dreams began each night before I ever closed my eyes.

Finally, all this story-telling began to show up in my life as writing. And while I've often felt lighter after writing in a journal or just freely putting my thoughts on paper, I never did so on a daily basis, never tied one day to the next, or one impression to another, the way memoir compels me to do. Writing memoir has helped me uncover pieces of myself that I had never wholly met.

Starting out in Madrid, 2004

In my late 30s, my professional life took me to Madrid, Spain where I lived, worked, and gathered stories as an expat; my memoir is comprised of these remarkable years.

Sarah Kegley

WHEN I WAS A CHILD, books attracted and transported me beyond the present, especially those in our family's living room. Around the fireplace, bookcases of Florida pine painted white reached nearly to the ceiling. On top sat four life-sized paper mache' masks from India—one with horns and another with a face like a tiger. In some cultures they protect homes from spooks, but not here. These curiosities reflected the artistic and bohemian spirits of our family—my sociologist father, political activist mother, me, and little sister Sally.

Often my posture for reading the big volumes and the local newspaper was kneeling with my forearms on the living room's rush mat. Mother pronounced my arched butt as unseemly. In yoga I've since learned it is a pose named for the graceful dolphin!

After retiring from Clark Atlanta University, I wanted to write about my parents—their interracial activities, my father's daring sociological research

Margaret (Peggy) and Winston (Dick) Ehrmann, Gretchen and Sally.

into college-student dating behavior, and my mother's Democratic Party activism in the 1950s. June Seese set me straight—I must write my own story. Exploring my rebellion in a segregated society that would drive me north, I recall my parents' spirit. With what my family calls my great memory, and referencing lots of letters, photographs, and memorabilia I have written my memoir.

Gretchen Ehrmann Maclachlan

MEMORY IS TICKLISH and quicksilver. Until my wife came across this photo, I had forgotten attending the Law Review editorial board's pre-graduation dinner in UVA's Rotunda. Then, bare bits and pieces flowed back with its aid, and were embellished. I recalled the strangeness of my being in the stark oval room, designed by Thomas Jefferson. Feeling hot in my winter suit, my only decent clothes, on a warmish May evening. I was surprised by my hubris in wearing a watch chain and ΦBK pin. I cannot recall what we ate, who served, or any conversations. I do recollect that Justice Lewis Powell addressed us, but not his subject. The picture reminded me strongly of how reassured I was to have Tracy with me through the novel social ritual. And I am pretty sure I remembered, sure enough to tell it, that as we emerged on the Lawn a full, white moon was ascending over the trees, and that it filled me with a thrill that our life together was a blank canvas, ready to be painted.

Jim Monacell

I SPENT MOST of my 35-year business career managing departments that were once labeled "Computers" and ultimately became "IT." Though the work called mostly for technical expertise, it also involved a good bit of writing, *e.g.*, operating procedures, user manuals, implementation plans. Priding myself on knowing and using a lot of words and on being able to put them together in conversations and documents as neatly and precisely as I could a line of programming code, I often volunteered to "do the writing."

Five years ago, I signed up for my first memoir writing class at Callanwolde, and I've been a regular in those classes ever since. They've taught me memoir writing skills that business writing has little use for—openness, creativity, flexibility, even experimentation. Though I've not made a smooth transition into these realms, I'm gradually getting comfortable. But I'm not about to stop trying. "Swimming" is about an experience that I began uncomfortably, but completed with satisfaction and pride. In a microcosm, that fifty-yard underwater swim at the story's end is what I hope memoir writing will become for me.

Bill Moore

In the great outdoors—where I like to be when I'm not writing.

When we have passed a certain age, the soul of the child we were and the souls of the dead from whom we have sprung come to lavish on us their riches and their spells.

Marcel Proust,
In Search of Lost Time

WRITING MY MEMOIRS was never of much interest to me, nor do I think my life—an unremarkable, garden-variety story if ever there was one—would be of much interest to anyone else. But I have been privileged to know some people whom I consider remarkable, for various reasons, and it is their stories that I believe are worth sharing. Their lives — their wisdom, foibles, sadness, and joys have enriched my own, and I am grateful that they have been my teachers. Though most of them are long dead now, writing their stories, which at best are merely snapshots, brings them back to life in a tangible way and reminds me of just how lucky I have been to know them.

Park Morgan

MY PARENTS, Abraham and Lillian Robinson Muskat, loved musical theatre. My brother Jeffrey and I grew up to the melodies of Richard Rogers and Jerome Kern. I was equally enchanted by Irving Berlin's clever rhymes and the pictures Oscar Hammerstein painted with his lyrics. From early on, I became a formidable rhymer.

But it was my 7th grade science teacher, Jerome Dework, who led me to pen and paper. He was of medium height, slightly paunchy and had a longish nose. Wisps of his light brown hair fell across his forehead. He stood at the front of the classroom behind a slate-topped lab table, where he kept a polished stone the size of a lime. Sometimes he bounced the stone on the table to make a point. In the upper left hand corner of the blackboard, he wrote a "quote of the day" by thinkers like Emily Dickinson or Albert Einstein. The sayings often had multiple meanings, and we began each class by discussing what they meant.

Mr. Dework's quotes taught me new ways of seeing the world and of seeing myself. They spoke of things I thought about but didn't yet know how to say. They made me feel less alone, and they inspired me to put my own words on paper—as I struggled to figure out who I was becoming.

Over the years, pens have turned into keyboards and paper to screens. Regardless, I've been writing as a way to make sense of my life ever since.

Lori R. Muskat

DURING THE DAY, I'm Senior Copywriter at The Studio, writing advertising for Synchrony Financial. Early mornings, evenings and weekends, I spend writing my memoir of my 48-year marriage: *We Thought We Would Live Forever (And for A While We Did)*.

The most valuable thing I've learned about writing, whether it's advertising or creative nonfiction is this:

> *What you leave out is more important than what you put in.*

Big thank-yous to June Seese, who showed me the way, and to my wife Danna, who keeps me on the path.

Robert Roth

AS A CHILD, I had a natural propensity for drama and never could quite rein in my imagination. For instance, I believed objects in my closet had feelings. When I picked out my clothes, I made sure to alternate different skirts or sweaters or slacks so that each had an equal share of out-of-the-closet time, and no one item felt ignored or unloved. When I reached for clothes, I could feel the material relax and smile in my small, six-year-old hands. My walks to and from my house to kindergarten and first grade were filled with made-up songs, skipping and original tales. Sometimes I would pretend that cracks were dangerous moats filled with alligators to be avoided. Sometimes I would run quickly, as my mind convinced me that I was being chased by a monster.

As an adult I was, as we all are, confronted by real-life monsters, such as the death of my father when I was twelve and the much-later dementia of my mother. I wanted to write so that I could sort out the beauty of the people I knew from the tragedy that old age brings. Writing helps when dealing with loss. You face the truth and look beyond your guilt, pain, and impotence.

Words allowed my grief to seep through the cracks of my heart. I learned to nurture the happy moments and understand the sad ones. I treasure the insights I have gained and hope others will find peace by seeing commonalities with their lives as well. Writing gives me the opportunity to heal, to remember, and to connect.

Shelley Scher

THIS PHOTO OF ME, my three siblings, my parents and my father's parents was taken in front of our house on Thornton Street in Hamden, Connecticut one month after I was born. In this house, ten years later, I listened to "Peggy Sue" and my other records in my attic bedroom.

Forty-two years later, this photo was taken, after my father had died and the house had been sold, when I visited the neighborhood with my wife, four-year old son and newborn daughter.

Paul R. Thim

Acknowledgments

We, the editors, gratefully acknowledge the following Callanwolde staff for their support of Callanwolde's writing program and of The Writing Room: Peggy Still Johnson - Executive Director; Nancy Sokolove- Arts Education Director; Jessica Miller - Marketing and Public Relations Director; Chip Kyle - Weekday Evening Facility Administrator; and Steve Cole - Arts Education Assistant. We thank also Chris Timmons for his assistance with the book's cover.